101 Questions & Answers on
THE HISTORICAL BOOKS OF THE BIBLE

Victor H. Matthews

Paulist Press
New York/Mahwah, NJ

Cover and book design by Lynn Else

Library of Congress Control Number: 2009938878

Published by Paulist Press
997 Macarthur Boulevard
Mahwah, New Jersey 07430

www.paulistpress.com

Printed and bound in the
United States of America

Contents

INTRODUCTION xi

THE 101 QUESTIONS AND ANSWERS

PART ONE: GENERAL QUESTIONS

1. What do we mean by the "historical books" of the Bible?....3

2. How did the ancients deal with the concept of history?.......3

3. Are the historical books divided into collections?..................4

4. Are there other historical books found elsewhere? 6

5. What do we mean by the "Deuteronomistic history"? 7

6. How does the Deuteronomistic history differ from
   the "Chronicler's history"? 8

7. How do we measure periods of history in the
   ancient Near East? 9

8. What can archaeology tell us about the history of
   ancient Israel? 10

9. What influence do topography and climate have on
   Israel's history? 11

10. Why do so many events in Israel's history occur
    at the same sites?...12

PART TWO: PRE-MONARCHIC ISRAEL

11. What evidence exists for the Exodus? 17

12. How many tribes were actually involved
in the Exodus?....................17

13. What role is played by the Sea Peoples in
Israelite history?....................18

14. What is the literary structure and plot of the
Book of Joshua?....................19

15. Is Joshua's account of the conquest and settlement
accurate?....................21

16. What evidence do we have of the settlement of the
Israelite tribes in the highlands of Canaan?....................22

17. What conclusions can be drawn about the Israelite
military campaigns in Canaan?....................23

18. What is the significance of Joshua's division of the
land and covenant renewal ceremony at Shechem?....................24

19. What is the literary structure and plot of the
Book of Judges?....................25

20. Why does the conquest narrative differ between
the Book of Joshua and the Book of Judges?....................27

21. What do the stories of the judges tell us about life
in pre-monarchic Israel?....................28

22. Are the judges role models for leadership in
ancient Israel?....................30

23. What weapons and warfare tactics were used by
the Israelites and their opponents?....................31

PART THREE: EARLY MONARCHY

24. What is the literary structure and plot of the
First Book of Samuel?....................35

25. What role did local shrines and the Ark of the
    Covenant play in pre-monarchy days? 36

26. What role did Samuel play in Israel's history? 38

27. What role do the Philistines play in the history
    of Israel? 39

28. Who are the Amalekites, and what role do they
    play in Israelite history? 41

29. Why do the people call on God and Samuel to
    give them a king? (1 Sam 8:1–15) 42

30. How was Saul chosen as king, and what role did
    he play as a war chief? 43

31. Why did Samuel challenge or condemn Saul's
    leadership on several occasions? 44

32. How does David become Saul's political rival? 46

33. How does David take advantage of his position
    as an outlaw? 47

34. What is the case against Saul's dynasty that allows
    David to become king? 49

PART FOUR: UNITED MONARCHY

35. What is the literary structure and plot of the
    Second Book of Samuel? 53

36. Why is it significant that David reigned first
    in Hebron? 54

37. What role does Joab play in the cycle of stories
    about David? 55

38. Why does David choose Jerusalem as his new capital
    city and then bring the Ark there? (2 Sam 5—6) 57

39. Did David really have an "empire"? 58

40. What is the significance of the "everlasting covenant"?
(2 Sam 7:8–17) 59

41. Was David an effective administrator and
military leader? 60

42. Why does Nathan tell David the parable of the
ewe lamb? (2 Sam 12:1–15) 60

43. What is the succession narrative, and what is
its significance? 61

44. What is the literary structure and plot of the
First Book of Kings? 63

45. How does Solomon become David's successor?
(1 Kgs 1—2) 64

46. How does Solomon earn the title "wise king"?
(1 Kgs 3; 4:29–34; 9:15–28; 10) 65

47. What products and natural resources contributed
to Israel's economy? 66

48. How do Ahijah's designation of Jeroboam and
Rehoboam's lack of diplomacy combine to create
a division in the kingdom? (1 Kgs 11:29—12:19)...............67

PART FIVE: DIVIDED MONARCHY

49. What role did Ammon, Moab, and Edom play in
Israel's history? 71

50. How do Judah and Israel differ, and how will this
affect their history? 72

51. Why are the actions taken by Jeroboam called
"Jeroboam's sin"? (1 Kgs 12:25–33)...............73

52. What "catch phrases" do the editors use in
chronicling the reigns of the kings? 74

53. What role does the Elijah and Elisha cycle of stories
play in the structure of Kings? 76

54. Why is Jezebel considered the worst woman in
Israel's history? 77

55. Why is Israel in constant conflict with Aram (Syria)? 78

56. What extra-biblical sources help with the
reconstruction of Israel's history? 80

57. What is the literary structure and plot of the
Second Book of Kings? 82

58. How does the message of Amos and Hosea relate
to Israel's history? 84

59. Who were the Assyrians, and what was their role
in Israel's history? 85

60. What role did Egypt play in Israel's history between
the tenth and sixth centuries BCE? 86

61. What are the results of the fall of Samaria in 721 BCE?
(2 Kgs 18:9–12) 88

62. How does First Isaiah's message relate to historical
events in Judah? 89

63. What is the result of Hezekiah's reform movement
in Judah? 90

64. What do the Siloam Inscription, Sennacherib's Assyrian
Annals, and the Rabshakeh's speech tell us about the
siege of Jerusalem? (2 Kgs 18:13–37; 20:20) 91

65. Why is Manasseh considered the worst king in
Judah's history? (2 Kgs 21:1–18) 92

66. What steps does Josiah take to centralize power and
    authority in Jerusalem? (2 Kgs 23:1–27) 93

67. How is Babylon able to come to power amid the
    ashes of the Assyrian empire? 94

68. How is Judah's growing instability depicted in the
    Second Book of Kings and in the Book of Jeremiah? 95

69. Why does Jeremiah counsel the people of Jerusalem
    to "accept the yoke of Babylon"? 96

70. What are the direct results of Nebuchadnezzar's
    capture of Jerusalem in 598? (2 Kgs 24) 97

71. How does the message of Ezekiel relate to events
    in Jerusalem? 98

72. Why do the people of Judah believe that God will
    never allow Jerusalem to be destroyed? 99

73. Why does Zedekiah revolt in 588, and what is the
    fate of Jerusalem in the following year? 100

74. Is Judah an empty land after the fall of Jerusalem? 102

PART SIX: EXILIC AND POSTEXILIC ISRAEL

75. What would life have been like for the exiles in
    Mesopotamia under Babylonian rule? 105

76. How did the exiles maintain their cultural identity
    while in Mesopotamia? 106

77. What led to Persia's rise and the expansion of its
    empire in the sixth century BCE? 107

78. How does Second Isaiah's message parallel the fall
    of Babylon to the Persians? 108

79. Did all of the exiles return to Palestine? 110

80. How did life in Palestine/Yehud change under Persian rule?....................111

81. How does the message of Haggai and Zechariah relate to events in Yehud?....................112

82. Why is there an eighty-year break in the chronicle of Israel's history after the Temple is restored?....................113

83. What role did Nehemiah play in the history of Yehud?....115

84. Who are the Samaritans?....................116

85. What role did Ezra play in the history of Yehud?............117

86. What is the literary structure and plot of the Books of Chronicles?....................118

87. How does the account of Israel's history in the Books of Samuel and the Books of Kings differ from that in Chronicles?....................119

88. Are First and Second Chronicles, Ezra, and Nehemiah a literary unit?....................121

PART SEVEN: HELLENISTIC AND ROMAN HISTORY

89. What do we know about Jewish communities outside of Yehud?....................125

90. What role does Alexander the Great play in the history of Israel?....................126

91. What is Hellenism?....................127

92. What influence did Hellenism have on Palestine?............128

93. What is the literary structure and plot of the Books of Maccabees?....................130

94. How did the struggles between the Ptolemies and Seleucids affect Israel's history?....................131

95. What were the causes and results of the
Maccabean Revolt?...133

96. How do the stories and visions in the Book of Daniel
relate to events in the Hellenistic period?.........................134

97. What do we know about the Hasmonean
rulers of Israel?...136

98. How do the Romans become the rulers of Palestine?.....137

99. What role is played by the Sadducees, Pharisees,
and Essenes?...138

100. What role does Herod play under Roman rule?.............139

101. Why did the Romans find it so difficult to
administer Palestine?...140

SELECT BIBLIOGRAPHY...143

Introduction

The volumes in the *101 Questions and Answers* series are designed to serve as a useful companion to a designated portion of biblical text. In this case, the focus is on the historical books and historical materials in the Bible. This particular volume contains commonly asked questions and provides nontechnical answers designed to assist laypeople, ministers, and students with a better understanding of the political, economic, and religious forces that dominated the world of ancient Israel. I begin with a few basic answers that provide an introduction to the character of history, historiography, archaeology, and environmental conditions in the ancient Near East. The remainder of the volume examines particular periods in the history of ancient Israel, starting with the premonarchical stories of the Exodus and the settlement period.

The transition to monarchy is explored in the Books of Samuel, and then attention is drawn to the establishment of the Davidic dynasty and the subsequent division of the kingdom into north and south. Particular attention is given to the roles of the major empires in Egypt and Mesopotamia and the growing influence they have on Israel and Judah. There is also an effort to identify and describe the role of Israel's neighbors (Ammon, Moab, Edom) and principal rivals (Amalekites, Philistines, Syrians). Caught in a vise of international intrigue, these two small nations eventually succumb to the political ambitions of their more powerful neighbors; both will be conquered and portions of their populations deported. With this turn of events, the answers turn to the exilic experience and the development of Jewish identity both in the countries of the exile and within the community of returnees in Jerusalem. The final sections then deal with Israel's relations with a succession of foreign masters, starting with the Persians and concluding with the Romans.

By necessity, the responses to the questions in this volume include many place-names and personal names. It is impossible to talk about history without describing the setting and the characters involved. I have provided insets to help ease the burden of so many names and to provide quick overviews of both historical events and of literary parallels in extra-biblical materials. Even so, it would be best to use this volume as a companion to your Bible and in conjunction with a biblical atlas and a Bible dictionary. A select list of reference works and related studies is found at the end of this book and serves as suggestions for further reading on this topic.

In every case, the answers in this volume are written as an aid to the layperson, minister, or religious professional. They are designed to allow you to gain a basic understanding of the biblical world and the history of ancient Israel. I have tried to avoid technical language where possible and when that was impossible— there are simply some terms that are necessary to biblical studies—I have provided definitions or explanations. It is my hope that this book will be used in a variety of educational settings. It is basic enough to be used in Bible study groups within church settings. Plus, it contains enough information that it could serve as a supplementary textbook in classes for the Bible as literature, introduction to the Hebrew Bible, or an introduction to the history of ancient Israel in university or seminary settings.

Wherever it is used, and whether by an individual or a group, I hope that the book will serve as an encouragement to deeper study of biblical materials.

PART ONE
General Questions

1. What do we mean by the "historical books" of the Bible?

While historical information is interspersed throughout the Bible (especially in the prophetic books), certain books within the canon have been identified as the traditional "historical books." Most recognizable of these are the books of Joshua through 2 Kings. They contain a fairly coherent and basically chronological recitation of events from the entrance of the Israelite tribes into Canaan under Joshua's leadership to the last days of the monarchy when the Babylonians destroy Jerusalem (587 BCE) and take a significant number of the people from Judah into exile.

Another rendition of some of this same material is also found in the First and Second Books of Chronicles, but there are some significant differences in the organization of events and in the manner in which some of the major characters are portrayed (see below, question 6). The prophetic books also contain information on kings, wars, and the fate of the Northern and Southern Kingdoms, but their primary focus, of course, is on the theological implications associated with these persons and events.

Finally, some information on life in ancient Israel after the exile is contained in the Books of Ezra and Nehemiah. They provide a partial glimpse of the difficulties and major social issues (intermarriage, Sabbath laws, competition with the Samaritans) that were faced by the returned exiles and their interaction with both the neighboring countries and the Persian imperial administration.

2. How did the ancients deal with the concept of history?

The modern conception of history is that it is an accurate accounting of true events within a defined period of time. While that may be a bit naïve, it reflects the Western notion of linear time in which a logical sequence of events takes place from antiquity and leading up to the present. In the ancient world, it was more common to think in terms of cycles and of remarkable events (reigns of kings or an earthquake; e.g., Amos 1:1). For instance, the Book of Judges contains a cyclical arrangement in which God responds to the unfaithfulness of the Israelites by allowing them to be oppressed by their neighbors. This, in turn, causes the people to cry out and acknowledge their need for God's help and God responds by "raising up" a judge, who temporarily provides the leadership needed to end the period of oppression. However, after the death of the judge, the people fall back into their sinful pattern and the cycle goes around again. In addition to this sense of the need to continually "return" to God, Israel's concept of history allows for a measure of flexibility in telling the story.

Differing traditions were interwoven in the editing process of the scriptures, reflecting the information one might expect about the rise of kings, significant battles, the construction of temples, and political relations with other nations. But it is also quite evident that the scribes responsible for recording this data chose to edit it in such a way that not every event is recorded, and a theological agenda is applied to demonstrate whether a king is good or bad. In other words, there is little attempt at objectivity since the most important aspect of the story is to explain the triumphs and failures of the nation in their relationship with God, rather than chronicling every detail during the course of Israel's history.

3. Are the historical books divided into collections?

It is not clear whether the ancient Israelites incorporated specific divisions into their canon of scriptures except in rather general terms: law, history, prophecy, and wisdom. The arrangement of the Bible today reflects our own desire for logical sequence and the identification of specific literary genres. As a result, the order of the

English canon is not the same as that of the Hebrew canon. In the latter, the text concludes with the Books of Ezra and Nehemiah, reflecting the tradition that Old Testament history and prophecy ends during the Persian period about 400 BCE. If we wish to define the actual periods of biblical history, they would include

—the ancestral narratives (Genesis 12—50)
—the Exodus and wilderness period (Exodus through Numbers)
—the settlement period (Joshua through Judges)
—the early monarchy period (1 and 2 Samuel through 1 Kings 11)
—the divided monarchy (1 Kings 12 through 2 Kings)
—the postexilic period (Ezra through Nehemiah)
—the intertestamental period (deuterocanonical books including 1 and 2 Maccabees)
—the Christian era (Gospels and Epistles)

By doing this it is possible to step through the history of the nation and get a sense of chronological order.

However, even though much of that history is contained in these groupings, it needs to be understood that additional information on the monarchy and postexilic periods is found in the prophetic books. In particular, the Books of Isaiah, Jeremiah, and Ezekiel provide good companions to the events recorded in the traditional historical books. For the New Testament period, only about a century is covered by the biblical text and none of the books are identified specifically as historical volumes. Instead, the history of the period serves as background to the development of the early church in the Near East and the Greco-Roman world during its formative stages.

4. Are there other historical books found elsewhere?

Since the biblical writers make reference to other historical works such as the Book of Jashar (Josh 10:13), the Annals of the Kings of Israel (1 Kgs 14:19), and the History of the Prophet Nathan (2 Chr 9:29), it may be assumed that there once existed a library of historical books from which to draw. However, none of these cited works are available to us now. This can be frustrating to us, but at least it indicates that the editors chose to draw on a set of rich traditions available in their own time.

The apocryphal or deuterocanonical books also contain historical books that add to the story of Israel's interaction with other nations. Thus, First and Second Maccabees provide some remarkable information on the Hellenistic period (c. 300–60 BCE) that answers many questions about the intertestamental era between the close of the Hebrew canon with Ezra (c. 400 BCE) and the beginning of the Christian era. In particular, there is a picture drawn of the culture wars in which traditional Jewish sects tried to maintain their identity in the face of a growing Hellenistic influence in Syria-Palestine. The triumph of the Maccabean rebels over their Greek Seleucid rulers and the creation of a short-lived Jewish state under the Hasmoneans (160–60 BCE) is one major highlight of these stories. These events are also chronicled in the writings of the Jewish historian Josephus (in his works *Jewish Antiquities* and *The Jewish War*), who attempted to create a history of the Jewish people down to the first century CE and the conquest of Jerusalem by the Romans. Again, however, neither the deuterocanonical books nor the work of Josephus are historical writing as we understand the term. Events are interpreted to advance theological, cultural, and political goals, and therefore these books are not considered to be particularly reliable sources for the history of the time.

5. What do we mean by the "Deuteronomistic history"?

Since the biblical text is a composite document that contains portions of oral tradition, legal pronouncements, historical chronicles, poetry, prophecy, and wisdom literature, it is a standard conclusion among scholars that several groups of editors at one time or another had a hand in creating what eventually became the canonical text of the Bible. One group collectively known as the "Deuteronomistic Historian" has been identified as responsible for much of the material contained in the books from Deuteronomy through 2 Kings. This so-called Deuteronomistic history contains distinctive and identifiably consistent vocabulary, syntax, themes, stylistic formulas, and a well-defined theological perspective on the events in Israelite history.

It is also clear from its emphasis on Jerusalem as the place where "God's name dwells"—and its generally positive presentation of the Davidic dynasty of rulers—that the Deuteronomistic Historian is a scribal voice from the Southern Kingdom of Judah. Almost none of the kings of the Northern Kingdom of Israel are identified as "good" kings: they continue to promote the "sin of Jeroboam" instead of obedience to the covenant with Yahweh (see question 51); they do not recognize Jerusalem as the cultic center for all Israelites; and they repeatedly engage in foreign wars and foreign alliances that contribute to the destruction of the nation and its people. Since the Deuteronomistic Historian is aware of the full range of events in Israel's history from the time of Joshua through the end of the monarchy, this material has been dated to the early sixth century BCE or during the exile later in that century. Its aim appears not only to provide a chronicle of events, but also to make it clear to the exilic audience that their current condition—stripped of their land, their king, and their Temple—is the direct result of their violation of the covenant and represents a just response by God. But hope also exists in this assessment of the past since it serves to guide future actions and assures the people that if they return to proper obedience to God's word and law, they can expect a restoration of their fortunes and a return to their homeland.

6. How does the Deuteronomistic history differ from the "Chronicler's history"?

The primary differences between the Deuteronomistic history and the Chronicler's account are based on when they were composed and their political and theological agendas. The Deuteronomistic history is generally considered to date to the end of the monarchy period or the early exilic era (early to mid-sixth century BCE). Its emphasis is on acknowledging the failures of the kings, the priests, and the people to obey the covenant and acknowledging the justification for God's allowing the nation to be conquered by Assyria and Babylonia. While there is a pronounced pro-Judahite and pro-Davidic tone to the Deuteronomistic history, it does not ignore the failings of David and Solomon or their successors.

The Chronicler's history, like the Books of Ezra and Nehemiah, is a fifth-century BCE composition that assumes a basic knowledge of the exilic experience and champions the restored priestly community of the Second Temple. One sign of this is the augmentation of the story of Solomon's bringing the Ark of the Covenant into the newly built Temple (1 Kgs 8:1–11). In the Chronicler's version (2 Chr 5:11–13), an extra section is added detailing the names of Levitical singers, the instruments they used, and the song of praise that formed part of the liturgical ritual. Since it is a truly retrospective account, the Chronicler presents a much more idealized version of events originally recorded in the Books of Samuel and Kings. For example, David's adultery with Bathsheba (2 Sam 11) does not appear in the Books of Chronicles, and Solomon's judgment of the two prostitutes (1 Kgs 3:16–28) is omitted. In another instance, 2 Kings 21:1–18 contains a list of King Manasseh's crimes and religious apostasies. However, the Chronicler's account portrays Manasseh as a repentant sovereign and reformer (2 Chr 33:12–16), who could not be blamed for Jerusalem's fall to the neo-Babylonians (compare 2 Kgs 21:10–15).

7. How do we measure periods of history in the ancient Near East?

The standard method of measuring periods of history in the ancient Near East is based on technology types: stone (Paleolithic and Neolithic) or copper (Chalcolithic), bronze, and iron. In the case of ancient Israel, it is based on dominant cultures or political situations: settlement, early monarchy, united monarchy, divided monarchy, exilic, postexilic. Of course, in particular areas of the Near East, these periods are tied to the local political situation as well. So in Egypt we speak of dynastic periods (Old Kingdom, Middle Kingdom, and New Kingdom), while in Mesopotamia, ethnic or cultural terms are used: Sumerian, Akkadian, Ur III or neo-Sumerian, Amorite, Assyrian, neo-Babylonian or Chaldean, and Persian.

For the purposes of the study of the ancient Israelites, the earliest period of history would be the Middle Bronze Age, which is associated with the ancestral narratives, the period of time in Egypt, and the Exodus. The settlement or conquest period occurs in the Iron Age I period, and the monarchy begins in Iron Age II-A. The divided monarchy spans the Iron Age II-B period, and the era of Judah's history prior to the Babylonian conquest occurs in Iron Age II-C. Once the exile begins, Israel's history is denoted by the imperial power that rules them. There is a brief period (142–60 BCE) during which a short-lived Jewish state (Hasmonean dynasty) rules in Jerusalem, but it is removed once the Romans expand their hegemony into Palestine. Jewish history effectively ends in Palestine in 135 CE after the Bar Kochva Revolt, when the Jews were forbidden to live within its boundaries. Thereafter, the history of the Jews radiates into many other countries and regions.

Middle Bronze II-A	c. 2000–1800/1750 BCE
Middle Bronze II-B/C	c. 1800–1550 BCE
Late Bronze I	c. 1550–1400 BCE
Late Bronze II	c. 1400–1200 BCE
Iron Age I	c. 1200–1000 BCE
Iron Age II-A	c. 1000–925 BCE
Iron Age II-B	c. 925–700 BCE
Iron Age II-C	c. 700–586 BCE
Neo-Babylonian Period	604–540 BCE
Persian Period	550–325 BCE
Hellenistic Period	325–60 BCE
Roman Period	60 BCE–135 CE

8. What can archaeology tell us about the history of ancient Israel?

Archaeology is one of several tools that are used to recon-struct the social world of ancient Israel. Architectural styles and building materials give us a sense of the way the ancients learned to cope with climatic conditions (temperature and annual rainfall), and how they made use of local topography (building on hillsides and terraces) and natural resources (lack of forests matched by an abundance of limestone quarries). The wealth of ceramic remains is an indication of technology (moving from hand-shaped to wheel-made pottery), of trade, of aesthetic tastes (glazes, decora-tion, shapes), as well as of the practical solutions to cooking, food and liquid storage, and lamps. Examination of burials provides information on concepts of the afterlife, personal identity, disease, diet, and average life spans.

Excavations can also help paint a picture of how the Israelites met the threat of warfare. City walls and complex gate areas, water tunnels, as well as the construction of sloped defenses (the glacis) speak to the need to prepare for a siege. Destruction levels with charred remains, the types of weapons used (sling stones, arrows, spears, swords), and mass graves point to the fact that these defenses were not always enough. What archaeology cannot do, however, is prove that the stories contained in the Bible are true. As a science, archaeology recovers and examines ancient artifactual remains, but its findings and conclusions are restricted to what has survived and that leaves a lot of holes in the story. Speculation about how a particular find relates to a particular biblical account is certainly possible, but it is not conclusive.

Values and Limitations of Archaeology

- While the material remains uncovered by archaeologists are incomplete, they provide our best available data upon which to create a partial reconstruction of life in ancient Israel.

- Interpretation of artifacts and excavation sites are subject to revision as new materials appear or new technologies are developed.

- As more sciences are incorporated into the archaeological process, more information can be obtained on ancient diet, farming and herding practices, disease, and forms of warfare.

- Archaeological remains are only one source of data used to interpret the Bible or to reconstruct the world of ancient Israel. However, they do represent the oldest artifactual remains available to us and as such deserve to be treated with respect and studied carefully.

- It is not possible to prove or disprove the truth of the biblical narrative using archaeological findings.

---

9. What influence do topography and climate have on Israel's history?

Physically, Canaan consists of several distinct topographic zones (coastal plain, Shephelah plateau, central hill country, Jordan valley, Negeb wilderness—see the list in Deut 1:7 and Jer 32:44) within a relatively small area (60 miles wide by 150 miles north to south). This allows for great variation in the types of settlement, architectural styles, ease of travel, political and social development, and the range of agricultural activities that are possible. In addition, Syria-Palestine enjoys a Mediterranean climate, with wet winter months (October to mid-April) and a dry summer (June to September).

God's blessings and the hope for a good harvest were often tied to having the rains fall in their season (Deut 11:14). The prevailing west wind comes off the Mediterranean Sea, bringing in weather fronts (1 Kgs 18:43–45), while a scorching east wind (the sirocco) causes dust storms, parches the ground, and withers the vegetation (Job 27:21–23; Ezek 17:10). To make the most of available moisture, the cultures of ancient Syria-Palestine developed hillside terracing, irrigation systems, and thick-walled architecture to moderate the temperatures. They also focused their farming economy on wheat, grapes, and olives. As might be expected, settlement initially centered on regions with higher annual rainfall or perennial water sources (springs and rivers), but with population growth and as a result of the invasion of the region by new peoples, such as the Philistines, new settlements appeared in the more mountainous or arid regions. So while topography and climate do not dictate every aspect of life, they do have significant influence on what is possible, including "seasons" of warfare (spring in 2 Sam 11:1), clothing styles, and trade routes.

10. Why do so many events in Israel's history occur at the same sites?

A close reading of the biblical narrative quickly demonstrates just how small the land of ancient Israel actually is (approximately 150 miles from north to south and 60 miles east to west at its widest point). Because of this geographic reality, the reader naturally will keep running into the same place-names. This is due in part to the fact that there were only a limited number of significantly sized cities and towns in ancient Syria-Palestine. Situated at strategic points, some like Megiddo guarded major crossroads, while others like Damascus took advantage of nearby trade routes. In those few cases where a major settlement appears off the beaten track, its origin is usually based on the exploitation of a particular natural resource (salt near the Dead Sea or copper at Khirbat en-Nahas in Edom) or a perennial water source (Jericho or Engedi).

As time went on, some of these well-placed population centers grew into cities that housed political leaders, temple communities, and prosperous merchants. Some also served as market hubs for the produce and products of the surrounding villages (called "daughters" in Ezek 16:46–55). Of course, given the frequent invasions of this region, no city managed to retain its importance throughout its history. For instance, Jericho's stratigraphy shows that its size and importance have fluctuated quite radically over its long history. While geography may have played a role in a city's being founded and contributed to its rise to prominence, natural disasters or political or economic shifts may in turn leave it a forgotten, backwater town or an abandoned ruin (e.g., Shiloh in Jer 26:6–9).

Shiloh Located in a fertile valley in the Ephraimite hill country between Shechem and Bethel (ten miles north of Bethel and twenty miles northeast of Jerusalem), just east of a trade route (Judg 21:19). Its fame originates with the story of Joshua's division of the land (Josh 18:1), its use as a cultic site where the Ark of the Covenant resides in Eli's time (1 Sam 4:3–4), and Jeremiah's reference to its ruins as a sign of God's displeasure (Jer 7:12–14; Ps 78:60).

Bethel Mentioned seventy-one times (second only to Jerusalem), the city is located twelve miles north of Jerusalem on the Ephraim-Benjamin border (Josh 16:2). It is tied to both Abraham (Gen 12:8) and Jacob (Gen 28:19) and is the site of one of King Jeroboam's two royal shrines (1 Kgs 12:32–33). Amos condemns the site and its priesthood (Amos 5:5–6). It is rebuilt by returning exiles during the Persian period (Ezra 2:28).

Jericho Situated fifteen miles northeast of Jerusalem near a powerful spring ('Ain es-Sultan), the city lays six miles west of the Jordan River and ten miles northwest of the Dead Sea in an artificially fertile plain. A Jordan River ford near the city links it to the trade route from Transjordan into the Judean hill country, extending westward to the coastal highway. It is linked to Joshua's conquest (Josh 2, 6), the judge Ehud's murder of the Moabite King Eglon (Judg 3:12–30), and Elijah's ascension (2 Kgs 2:4–5).

PART TWO

Pre-Monarchic Israel

11. What evidence exists for the Exodus?

Other than the biblical account of the Exodus, we do not have any written or archaeological evidence that is conclusive proof that it actually occurred. However, there are some indications that do point to some aspects of the story. For instance, there is mention in the royal annals of Pharaoh Ramesses II (1304–1237 BCE) of the two storehouse cities—Pithom and Ramesses—constructed by the Israelite slaves (Exod 1:11). The pharaoh does not explicitly state that they were constructed by Israelites, but it is fairly common to find mention of "Asiatic" workers in Egyptian texts.

In addition, the alternative route of the Exodus, designed to avoid open warfare along the "Way of the Philistines" (Exod 13:17), suggests that a string of fortresses was constructed along this coastal road that connected Egypt with Canaan. Recent archaeological excavations on this land bridge have produced several Egyptian outposts that date to the thirteenth century BCE. Finally, a monumental inscription produced for Pharaoh Merneptah (1213–1204 BCE)—which contains an account of a military expedition into Canaan and lists the various cities and peoples conquered by the Egyptian forces—includes the ethnic term *Israel*. This provides an indication that the Israelites were in Canaan by 1208 BCE, giving a terminus date for the Exodus from Egypt. Ultimately, the importance placed on the Exodus throughout the Bible as the great saving-event for ancient Israel, as well as a fulfillment of God's obligation to the covenant people, suggests that this tradition has some basis in fact despite a lack of sufficient extra-biblical, historical data.

12. How many tribes were actually involved in the Exodus?

Although the assumption in the biblical narrative is that all twelve Israelite tribes participated in the Exodus, the only full list of Jacob's sons is found in the prologue to the Book of Exodus when they first *entered* Egypt (Exod 1:1–5). No similar list occurs at the time that the Israelites are said to have *left* Egypt. Instead of mentioning them all by name, collective terms are used: *the people* (Exod 13:17–18); the *companies of the LORD* (Exod 12:41), and the *whole congregation* (Exod 16:1). Furthermore, there is little reference to the activities or the leaders of these tribes except in those instances when they either assist (seventy elders appointed in Exod 18:25–26 and Num 11:16–30) or challenge Moses' leadership (Korah's Revolt in Num 16:1–3).

Only when Moses sends twelve spies into Canaan (Num 13:1–15) is there a full listing once again of all the participating tribes. Of course, the one tribe most intimately tied to the Exodus tradition is the tribe of Levi, with Moses and Aaron as its most prominent members. The tribe of Judah is represented by Caleb, one of the twelve spies and the only man other than Joshua (from the tribe of Ephraim) to survive the wilderness wanderings (Num 13:6; 14:6–9). Since the biblical record of the Exodus is composed long after the event, and some tribal traditions may not have been preserved, the editors may have felt more comfortable simply referring to the "Israelites" rather than constantly listing each tribe by name. In addition, the importance of the tribes of Judah, Levi, and Ephraim during the monarchy period necessitates their prominence in the Exodus narrative.

13. What role is played by the Sea Peoples in Israelite history?

The cultures and the political status of the Levant (Syria-Palestine and the eastern Mediterranean area) are disrupted around 1200 BCE by mass, armed invasions of Egypt, Syria-Palestine, and Anatolia by groups collectively known as the Sea Peoples. The Egyptian Pharaoh Ramesses III (1184–1150 BCE) left written records and temple reliefs depicting how the Sea Peoples were defeated in naval and land battles, but other areas were not as lucky.

For example, the important seaport city of Ugarit in northern Syria was destroyed by the invaders, leaving an economic and political vacuum that is eventually filled by the Phoenicians and their Mediterranean seaports at Tyre and Sidon. The Hittite kingdom in Anatolia is also defeated by the Sea Peoples and was never able to recover. This in turn allowed encroachment on their territory by the Assyrian and Amorite dynasties in northern Mesopotamia. Egyptian hegemony over Canaan was severely affected, although archaeological evidence suggests that the Egyptians continued to maintain at least an economic presence there.

Most important to the history of the Israelites, however, was the defeat of the Canaanite cities in the coastal region and on the Shephelah plateau by the branch of the Sea Peoples known as the Philistines. These invaders established themselves in five major city-states (Gaza, Ashkelon, Ashdod, Ekron, and Gezer) and dominated the adjoining area with their superior military technology (1 Sam 13:19–21). The forced migrations of Canaanites combined with the appearance of new ethnic groups (including the proto-Israelites) and opened up new settlements in previously uninhabited or sparsely inhabited areas of the central hill country of Canaan. During the period from 1200 to 1000 BCE, these peoples created social and cultural identities for themselves and struggled to compete with the Philistines. Most important, however, was the fact that the superpowers of Egypt, Anatolia, and Mesopotamia were not actively involved in Syria-Palestine during this period and that allowed for the development of new states, including Israel.

14. What is the literary structure and plot of the Book of Joshua?

The Book of Joshua consists of five distinct sections:

1. Entrance into the Promised Land (1:1—5:12)
2. Conquest of Canaan (5:13—11:23)

3. Distribution of the land to the Israelite tribes
   (12:1—19:51)
4. Allotment of tribal lands in Gilead and a threat of civil
   war (20:1—22:34)
5. Joshua's farewell address and covenant renewal
   (23:1—24:33).

The principal themes and plot of the Book of Joshua include the theological viewpoint that obedience to Yahweh's command brought prosperity and military success. Other themes and plot points are Joshua's emergence as Moses' successor, the major campaigns under Joshua's leadership that brought Canaan under Israelite control, and the establishment of tribal boundaries so that all Israelites and their descendants have a portion of the Promised Land as a sign of their membership in the covenant community. If this account of the conquest is compared to that found in the Book of Judges, it is easy see that it is an idealized and very theological rendition of events. Every military campaign is a complete success, no matter what odds or weapons technology (horses and chariots; Josh 11:4) that the Israelites face.

Only when Achan disobeys God's instruction to commit all of the people, animals, and property of the inhabitants of Jericho to the *herem* (total destruction as a sacrifice to God) do they have a setback in their next battle at Ai (Josh 7). Once the lawbreaker and his family are executed and the congregation is purified of this sin, the string of victories resumes. The systematic division of the land provides a geographically inclusive framework for national as well as tribal identity, but it too is idealized since the Israelites will still have to compete with the Philistines and Canaanites for the use and ownership of the land. Joshua's final admonition and warning to remain obedient and faithful to God (Josh 23:14–16) sets a tone that culminates in a mass assembly at Shechem in which the people pledge their allegiance and are then sent to occupy their individual holdings (Josh 24:19–28).

15. Is Joshua's account of the conquest and settlement accurate?

The object of the conquest narrative in the Book of Joshua is to demonstrate the theological principle that God will give the chosen people victory over their opponents as long as they remain obedient and do not serve other gods. The result is an idealized account that glorifies Joshua's leadership in a series of military campaigns that encompasses the entirety of Canaan and leads to the utter defeat of a long list of kings. The injection of miraculous intervention by Yahweh, the Divine Warrior, in the capture of Jericho (Josh 6) and of the miraculous lengthening of the day in the campaign against the Amorites of the hill country (Josh 10:1–15) serves the Deuteronomistic Historian's theological agenda, which is not particularly concerned with providing a realistic account of the battles. In addition, archaeologists have found no physical evidence for the conquest and destruction of most of the cities listed in the narrative during the time period associated with the stories.

Jericho was not a major walled city during the twelfth century BCE and the once thriving city of Ai was an uninhabited ruin during that period. In fact, none of the sites mentioned as part of the conquest narrative have destruction levels that can be directly associated with Joshua and the Israelites. Certainly, there were periods of warfare and the attendant destruction it brings, but this destruction cannot be conclusively proven to be part of an Israelite conquest of the land. As far as the relationship between the settlement of the land and the account of the division of the Promised Land among the Israelite tribes are concerned, this also is an idealized portrayal of events. In fact, the archaeological record suggests that the Israelites were confined to the hill country until the establishment of the monarchy. Therefore, the most likely conclusion to be drawn is that the account in the Book of Joshua is designed to serve the political purposes of the later monarchy and to provide a theological underpinning for the Deuteronomistic Historian's equation: obedience and faithful = God's protection and blessing.

16. What evidence do we have of the settlement of the Israelite tribes in the highlands of Canaan?

Excavations and surveys in the central highlands of Canaan (between Jerusalem and the Valley of Jezreel) demonstrate a dramatic growth in the population between 1150 to 1000 BCE. Hundreds of new villages (100 to 250 people each) sprang up in previously uninhabited areas. This occupation area was framed by the Philistine city-states that controlled the coastal plain and the Shephelah and the remnants of Egyptian trading centers, Canaanite cities, and newly established Philistine cities on the northern coast and in the Jezreel corridor from Megiddo to Beth-shan. In order to survive in the less hospitable region of the hill country, agricultural production was adapted to soil types and rainfall amounts. Harvests and the number of agricultural products were expanded by the labor-intensive construction of terraces (10 to 15 feet wide) on hillsides (see Isa 5:1–6) and by the carving of water cisterns into the soft limestone bedrock. There is also evidence of a mixed economy blending sheep and goat herding with the cultivation of wheat and legumes, the tending of vineyards, and the planting of olive trees, thereby increasing the chances for survival in a region marked by drought three years out of every ten.

Although some would suggest that new and distinctive architecture (the four-room house) and pottery types (collared rim jars) are to be associated with the entrance of the Israelite tribes into the highlands, the case has not been adequately proven. Given the mention of the ethnic term *Israel* in the Egyptian Merneptah stele (c. 1208 BCE), it is apparent that a defined group of people bearing that name existed during this time period. However, it is also quite likely that they shared the highlands with other migrants, including Canaanites who had been driven out of the coastal plain and the Shephelah plateau by the Philistines. The history of the settlement is therefore a history of the close association, probably including intermarriage and cultural sharing, between ethnic groups who eventually coalesced into what would be known as the nation of Israel.

17. What conclusions can be drawn about the Israelite military campaigns in Canaan?

The accounts of military campaigns in the Book of Joshua fall into two categories. First, there are stories about the Divine Warrior who gives the underdog Israelites miraculous victories. This includes the capture and destruction of Jericho that is accomplished, not by military strategy or siege engines, but by obedience to the divine command to process around the city walls and then at an appointed time shout for divine intervention, which arrives with devastating effect. Even the elements of creation are altered to give the Israelites a victory over the Amorites when the Lord caused the sun to "stand still" (Josh 10:12–13). In another case, the Israelites are faced with a massive army, including swarms of horse-drawn war chariots which are led by a coalition of kings (Josh 11:1–5). This formidable enemy force is "handed over" to the Israelites by their God, who assures Joshua that he need not be afraid and then joins in the rout of the surprised enemy (11:6–9).

The other type of military account provides a glimpse of how the Israelites overcame their foe by using subterfuge rather than standard military tactics. In these cases, as in the capture of Ai, victory comes as a result of an ambush that draws the defenders away from their walls and allows a second Israelite force to seize the city (Josh 8:3–23). It is sometimes difficult to picture how these events transpired since the descriptions of troop movements are not comprehensive. But there are instances in which it is possible to envision a scene such as the humiliation of the coalition of five kings, who were forced to the ground and had to submit to the indignity of having a foot placed on their neck (Josh 10:24). It should be kept in mind in reading these accounts that the magnitude of these battles, the size of the armies, and the vast number of soldiers slaughtered in these battles are clearly exaggerated. Only major nations marshaled armies of 30,000 men, and yet the Israelites are said to have fielded even more than this. More important than strict attention to exact detail for the editors of these accounts is their desire to demonstrate the power of Yahweh over the gods of Canaan in this struggle for control of Canaan.

18. What is the significance of Joshua's division of the land and covenant renewal ceremony at Shechem?

The original covenant promise that Yahweh made to Abram (Gen 12:1–2; see Gen 15:18–21 for a more explicit statement) offered land and children in exchange for obedience and exclusive worship. From that point, each subsequent reiteration of the covenant promise contained these elements and reinforced the importance of land for a state-less people (Gen 28:13–14). In particular, Genesis 17:4–8 confirms that "all the land of Canaan" will be their "perpetual holding." Then, when God took a hand to release the Israelites from their enslavement in Egypt (compare the prediction in Gen 15:13–14 and God's statement to Moses in Exod 3:17), the goal for the people was to reach the Promised Land and take possession. Unfortunately, that goal was delayed by their disobedience and by the subsequent period of wandering in the wilderness (Num 14:1–24).

The recitation of the conquest narrative in the Book of Joshua thus becomes a testament to God's faithfulness in keeping the covenant promise. It is further certified by Joshua's renewal of the covenant during an assembly of the people at Shechem (Josh 24). His choice of location is important since Shechem was the first place that Abram stopped on his arrival in Canaan and worshipped Yahweh (Gen 12:6–7). Plus, he models this ceremony after the one conducted by Moses at Mt. Sinai (Exod 24:1–8), thus bringing the full Exodus and conquest to an end. With the conflict over, Joshua's division of the land stands as the culmination of the covenant promise, assuring each Israelite household membership in the covenantal community as a landholder. The strength of this tradition is found centuries later in the firm refusal of Naboth to sell his land to King Ahab because it would strip his descendants of their "ancestral inheritance" (1 Kgs 21:3).

Of course, there are also political implications to this division since it established the boundaries of the tribal territories. Some of these boundaries did shift, given the realities of the political situation in Canaan (the tribe of Dan is forced to migrate north when they cannot coexist with their Philistine neighbor; Judg 18). When the monarchy is established, the kings will have to find ways to create a sense of national identity that will transcend local, tribal identities (see Solomon's administrative structure in 1 Kgs 4:7–19).

19. What is the literary structure and plot of the Book of Judges?

It is clear that the Book of Judges originated as unrelated stories that were recounted in oral form and subsequently compiled and edited into a fairly coherent document. The collection has two main purposes:

1. A depiction of the political and social chaos of the Judges period, serving as an argument for the establishment of the monarchy and the need to rely on Yahweh
2. A polemic against the illegitimate rulers in the Northern Kingdom, justifing the legitimacy of the Davidic dynasty in Judah

The Book of Judges begins with a general introduction that attempts to provide a transition following Joshua's death and the chaotic conditions that then necessitate the "raising" of judges. What follows in chapters 3 through 16 are the exploits of these judges as they attempt to relieve the Israelites of the burden of oppression by their neighbors. This section is developed around a framework cycle containing the recurrent phrase, "the Israelites again did what was evil in the sight of the LORD." Each time this phrase occurs it signals that the cycle of Israelite disobedience has begun again and by necessity requires God to allow them to fall once again into oppression until they repent and call out for divine help. The final chapters (17–21), which do not contain stories of judges, provide a poignant theme characterized by the recurrent phrase, "in those days there was no king in Israel; all the people did what was right in their own eyes" (Judg 18:1; 21:25). Ultimately, the fact is hammered home to the audience that the Israelites, despite having a judge raised to assist them, always resume the pattern of disobedience that causes God's displeasure.

Judges Framework Cycle

(1) The people of Israel do "evil in the sight of the LORD" (2:11; 3:7, 12a; 4:1; 6:1a; 10:6; 13:1a).

(2) Yahweh's anger leads to oppression of the Israelites by their neighbors (2:14; 3:8, 12b; 4:2; 6:1b; 10:7; 13:1b).

(3) When the Israelites repent and call upon Yahweh, God "raises up" a judge to deliver them from their oppressors (2:16; 3:9b, 15b).

(4) Following a period of peace, the death of the judge marks a return to Israel's pattern of unfaithfulness and the cycle resumes.

There are a few stories that do not fit the framework cycle, such as Shamgar's heroics (3:31) and the lists of "minor judges" (10:1–5 and 12:8–13). The only extended narrative outside the framework is the story of Abimelech ben Jerubbaal (chapter 9), which is appended to the Gideon narrative and serves as a prime example of why illegitimate rulers come to a bad end. The final five chapters (17—21) ratchet up the level of violence and the sense of a society without legal constraints. It also lacks the leadership of judges to mitigate some of this madness. Curiously, the heroic tales of the judges never drew all of the tribes together in a common cause, but in these final chapters, idolatry, theft, and rape at last draw all of the tribes together into a civil war. The book concludes with the plaintive cry, "there was no king in Israel" (Judg 21:25).

20. Why does the conquest narrative differ between the Book of Joshua and the Book of Judges?

The most direct answer to this question is that the purpose or theme of each of these books is different. The Book of Joshua provides an idealized narrative that allows the Israelites to complete a clean sweep of Canaan based on their obedience to God's command and on the direct intervention of the Divine Warrior to insure their military victories. The only halt in an otherwise glorious string of successes is based on Achan's theft from the property consigned to the *herem* at Jericho (Josh 7). Once he has admitted his guilt and been punished, the people are purified of their sin and can resume their task unabated and with great fervor (Josh 8:1–29).

While the Book of Judges also records Yahweh's role in a number of military campaigns, these are local battles, and in most cases they represent the activities of the judges that have been raised by God to deal with oppressors. Thus, Gideon's depleted army of 300 is able to defeat a Midianite army that covered a valley "like locusts," with God's help and the element of surprise (Judg 7:2–23). Judges also contains more realistic accounts and assessments of events that provide mundane explanations for the Israelites' failure to complete the conquest of Canaan. For instance, even though the tribe of Judah is successful in capturing control over the southern portion of the hill country allotted to them, they are unable to conquer the "people of the plain" because they have superior technology, "iron chariots" (Judg 1:19; compare Joshua's victory in 11:6–9 over an army with iron chariots). The Book of

Judges even includes two very curious explanations for why God allowed some of the peoples of Canaan to survive the Israelite invasion. One reason follows the pattern set in the Book of Joshua: that the Israelites must maintain complete fidelity to Yahweh in order to obtain success. But this is given an extra twist in the Book of Judges where the Canaanites remain as a sort of "test" to determine "whether or not they would take care to walk in the way of the LORD as their ancestors did" (Judg 2:22). The second explanation for the continued survival of the Canaanites is based on God's desire to provide the Israelites with practical lessons in warfare (Judg 3:2). Of course, these are rationalizations, but the viewpoint of the editors is more reflective of the political and social situation during the late monarchy period rather than the time of the settlement. In both accounts, Yahweh is distinguished as the real power capable of removing Israel's oppressors. In both it is the faithfulness of the Israelites that is being tested. However, the Joshua narrative does not focus on anything but the accomplishment of God's plan, while in Judges a case is being made for the establishment of a monarchy that can end the chaos and idolatry and help lead the people into an era of obedience to law and an appreciation of order.

21. What do the stories of the judges tell us about life in pre-monarchic Israel?

There are three main things that can be inferred from the stories in the Book of Judges:

1. Society is centered around small farming villages in the central hill country whose survival is threatened by their predatory and technologically superior neighbors.
2. Kinship and membership in the tribe dominate political and economic life because there is no central government or national leader (the judges are local heroes).
3. Religion is local and consists of a mixture of Yahweh worship and Canaanite practice.

The first inference is based on the frequency with which the Israelite tribes are oppressed (raided, plundered, and/or forced to pay tribute) by the Moabites (Judg 3:13–15), the Canaanites (Judg 4:2–3), the Midianites (Judg 6:1–6), the Ammonites (Judg 10:6–9), and the Philistines (Judg 15:11–13). The theological explanation for these miseries is the unfaithfulness of the Israelites, "who did what was evil in the sight of the LORD, worshiping the Baals and the Astartes" and the gods of other nations (Judg 6:6). In fact, without strong and consistent leadership, the Israelite tribes and their small villages were easy prey for better armed and organized bands of raiders. Short term, these marauders would rape and pillage, and then settle in to bleed the villagers dry of their crops and animals. This explains Gideon's attempt to hide his grain by beating it into flour in a wine press (Judg 6:11). Kept weak, the Israelites were no threat unless a local war chief (meaning a judge) could organize a resistance and drive the foreign oppressors out, at least for a time.

The second inference—the importance of kinship and tribal affiliation as the dominant social glue in this period—is found in the inability of even the most dynamic of the judges to pull together all of the tribes to meet a crisis. Deborah's song (Judg 5) decries the poor excuses supplied by some tribes who refuse to join Barak's army. Furthermore, the tribes cause themselves further grief by fighting among themselves. Both Gideon's and Jephthah's tribal forces have to stave off potential (Judg 8:1–3) and real military aggression by their fellow tribesmen from Ephraim (Judg 12:1–6). And, Gideon's renegade son Abimelech sets himself up as a warlord with the help of his mother's kinship group in Shechem and then proceeds to ravage nearby towns as well as Shechem before he is brought to a shameful end, when a millstone is dropped on his head by a woman (Judg 9).

The last inference—that Yahweh worship is mixed with Canaanite practice—is also apparent during the judges period. Gideon is commanded by God to tear down an altar to Baal that his father had constructed in their village. Fearing reprisals by the villagers, he does it in the dead of night and still has to face their wrath the next day (Judg 6:25–32). Jephthah makes a foolish vow, hoping to obtain a military victory with God's help, and is forced to keep his word and to sacrifice his only daughter (Judg 11:30–40), a clear violation of the precedent banning human sacrifice in Abraham's time (Gen 22:1–14). Topping off the evidence of unfaithfulness is the incredible story of Micah's idol. An Ephraimite steals silver from his mother, and when he returns it, she has part of it fashioned into an idol. Her son then creates a household shrine for the image and hires a Levite to officiate before it. It is finally stolen and his Levite hired away by the migrating tribe of Dan, which sets up the idol in their newly captured city of Dan (Judg 17—18). In this linked tale, the sin of one man eventually becomes the failure of an entire tribe, but then in that time, "Everyone did what was right in their own eyes" (Judg 21:25).

22. Are the judges role models for leadership in ancient Israel?

In times of uncertainty, lawlessness, and violence, it is not surprising to find the judges put forward as role models, who may spark the courage and determination of the Israelites to resist their oppressors. Some, like Othniel (Judg 3:7–11) and Deborah (Judg 4—5), could be said to provide the ethical leadership needed in this period, but they are the exception. It is much more common for these local heroes to be depicted as tricksters (murderous, left-handed Ehud with his concealed dagger, Judg 3:16–23), reluctant generals (Barak, who fears to proceed with the prophetess Deborah, Judg 4:4–8; Gideon who demurs when called to serve, Judg 6:12–15, and tests God's intentions, Judg 6:36–40), and self-indulgent, shortsighted warriors (Samson and Jephthah). It would be hard to point to Samson's sexual escapades, violent tendencies, and lack of guile as true exemplars of leadership or proper behavior (Judg 14—16).

Of course, the exaggerated nature of hero tales and the bigger-than-life appetites and activities of these individuals are part of the literary genre of epic and legend. The stories are also entertaining and, in the end, the heroes do manage, with God's help, to defeat Israel's enemies and bring temporary periods of peace to some of the tribal territories. The crisis-based leadership of the judges reflects the need to organize the people's efforts and will eventually result in the emergence of war chiefs, like Saul and David, and eventually the establishment of the monarchy in ancient Israel.

23. What weapons and warfare tactics were used by the Israelites and their opponents?

Throughout the stories in the Book of Judges, the Israelites are portrayed as incapable of defeating their enemies without God's direct intervention and because they lacked the quality and quantity of weapons possessed by their oppressors. This graphically displays how technologically poor the material culture of the Israelites was in this period and plays up the underdog theme that makes a victory even more astonishing. It also helps explain why they must admit that they "could not drive out the inhabitants of the plain, because they had chariots of iron" (Judg 1:19).

Balancing such deficiencies are the judges raised by God to provide models of courage and resistance or even to provide entertainment during the dark days of their oppression by more dominant cultures. Thus, when Shamgar is capable of killing 600 Philistines with the sharpened stick (his ox goad) that he uses to manage his animals' movements (Judg 3:31), and when Samson strikes down the Philistines "hip and thigh with great slaughter" (Judg 15:8) or kills a thousand with the "fresh" jawbone of a donkey (Judg 15:15–16), the Israelite audience would applaud. Similarly, the Israelite battle tactics tend to focus on ambushes, night attacks, and, of course, the softening up of the enemy by the Divine Warrior (Judg 4:14–16). This makes perfect sense because the Israelites are outnumbered and the enemy can deploy not only a host of well-armed fighters but also has iron chariots and camels.

Judge	Weapon	Opponent's Weapon	Warfare Tactic
Ehud (Judg 3:12–30)	Two-edged "sword" 18 inches long, hidden under clothing (3:16)		Assassinates King Eglon with hidden weapon (3:16–23)
Shamgar (Judg 3:31)	Oxgoad		
Deborah (Judg 4)		900 chariots of iron (Judg 4:3)	
Gideon (Judg 7)	Trumpets, jars, and torches (7:16–20)	Countless soldiers and camels (7:12)	Night attack, confusion, and noise (7:19–22)
Abimelech (Judg 9)	Upper millstone flung from besieged city (9:53)		Ambushes (9:32–43); fire to weaken city walls (9:48–49)
Samson (Judg 15—16)	Jawbone of donkey (15:15–16)		

PART THREE

Early Monarchy

24. What is the literary structure and plot of the First Book of Samuel?

The First Book of Samuel provides a transition from the political and social chaos of the judges period to the beginning of the monarchy, including the tragedy of Saul's reign and the rise of David. Of particular importance here is Samuel's role as judge-prophet-priest. His tale begins with his miraculous birth to an infertile mother (1 Sam 1:1–20) and continues with his apprenticeship as a priest at Shiloh (1 Sam 1:26–28), his call by God (1 Sam 3:1–18), and his emergence as the unquestioned leader of the people within his judicial circuit in the central hill country (1 Sam 3:19–21; 7:3–17).

The model of temporary leadership found in the Book of Judges now proves to be unsatisfactory, and the people clamor for a king to rule them (1 Sam 8:1–5). This provides the second major thread of the First Book of Samuel—the arguments for and against a king (1 Sam 8:6–18). Ultimately, it is God who instructs Samuel to seek out the proper candidate and anoint him as God's chosen ruler over the Israelites. This brings Saul into the picture, although the narrative provides a mixed picture of his character. This mixture of attitudes (compare the very positive picture of Saul in 1 Sam 9—10:16 with the extremely negative portrayal in 1 Sam 10:17–27) may reflect the conflicts that will exist within Israelite society and among the editors of this narrative throughout the monarchy period. Although Saul does prove himself in battle and receives the formal allegiance of the tribal elders (1 Sam 11), he almost immediately begins to have problems balancing the need to preserve the people from the threat of the Philistines and Samuel's insistence that Saul strictly obey God's instructions (1 Sam 13—15). When Saul fails to do this, Samuel is instructed to seek out another candidate for the kingship. It is at this point that David is introduced and the long path to the throne begins for the shepherd boy (1 Sam 16:1–14).

The remainder of the First Book of Samuel is the account of Saul's political and personal disintegration, and the emergence of David as God's anointed and the hope for the people. Interspersed within this narrative are subplots, the most important of which is David's respect for the person of the "LORD's anointed" and his refusal to participate in the death of Saul (see 1 Sam 24:1–7; 26). Major plot details in what is known as the "apology" or the sympathetic tale of David are his triumph over the giant Goliath (1 Sam 17), David's outlaw period when he must hide from Saul's wrath but uses the time to gather a following of men and supporters throughout the country (1 Sam 19:8–26), and David's time as a mercenary chief, pretending to serve the Philistines while gaining wealth and military expertise that will assist him when he becomes king (1 Sam 27). The book ends with Saul's desperate questioning of the witch of Endor and his final battle at Gilboa (1 Sam 28 and 31).

25. What role did local shrines and the Ark of the Covenant play in pre-monarchy days?

The Israelites had not established a central shrine during the pre-monarchic period. Because the tribes were not united and communication between the various sections of Canaan was not continuous, it is not surprising that several sites, including Shechem, Bethel, Gilgal, and Shiloh, had cultic importance and were associated with religious activity in this period. But none was able to gain preeminence. Also during this period, the Ark of the Covenant appears prominently only during the conquest of Canaan when it is carried at the head of procession by the Levites or into battle (Josh 3—4, 6—8). At the end of the pre-monarchic era, it resides at Shiloh and is ministered to by a family of Levitical priests lead by Eli (1 Sam 1:3; 3:3).

Although the Ark was originally constructed to house the tablets of the Law (Exod 25:10–22) and to serve as a reassurance of

God's presence with the people in the wilderness, it takes on a more martial character during the conquest. What is apparently not clear to the Israelites, however, is that God the Divine Warrior is not obligated to fight for them when they have not remained faithful. As a result, when the call is made to have the Ark carried into battle against the Philistines, the sins of Eli's sons justify God's abandonment of the Israelites (1 Sam 4:1–11). The Ark is captured, held as hostage before the god of the Philistines, and then liberates itself when God sends a plague, causing the Philistines to send it away. Without Levites to care for the Ark (Eli and his sons have all died; 1 Sam 4:11–18), the Ark is seen as too dangerous to handle and is stored at Kiriath-jearim (1 Sam 6:19—7:2) and will not emerge again until David's time.

Cultic Sites in the Pre-Monarchic Period

Shechem Located approximately thirty miles north of Jerusalem and dominated by the twin peaks of Mt. Ebal and Mt. Gerizim, Shechem's traditional authority is attached to Abram's initial entrance into Canaan and the construction of an altar near here (Gen 12:6–7). It is also the site of Joshua's covenant renewal ceremony following the conquest (Deut 11:29; Josh 24).

Shiloh Shiloh is strategically located between Shechem and Bethel (ten miles north of Bethel and twenty miles northeast of Jerusalem). It is first highlighted when Joshua assembles the people here for the division of the land (Josh 18:1); its cultic importance is associated with the Ark of the Covenant that resides there in Eli's time (1 Sam 4:3–4).

Bethel Located twelve miles north of Jerusalem on the Ephraim-Benjamin border, Bethel is tied to both Abram (constructs an altar; Gen 12:8) and Jacob (experiences a theophany and covenant promise; Gen 28:19). During the civil war between the Israelite tribes, they go to Bethel to ask for guidance from God and to sacrifice (Judg 20:18, 26).

Gilgal Situated just north of Jericho near the Jordan River, Gilgal is the first encampment after the Israelites enter Canaan to begin the conquest (Josh 4:20). It is here that the people celebrate the first Passover in the Promised Land (Josh 5:10–11). It is one of the three places, along with Bethel and Mizpah, where Samuel sat as judge (1 Sam 7:16) and is the site where Saul is proclaimed king (1 Sam 11:14–15).

26. What role did Samuel play in Israel's history?

In much the same manner as Moses does during the Exodus and wilderness period, Samuel plays multiple roles in the transition period between the settlement era and the monarchy. Also like Moses (Exod 2:1–10), he has a miraculous birth narrative that sets him apart as a future leader of his people (1 Sam 1:1–20). He is a judge, a priest, and a prophet—called by God to all of these offices (1 Sam 3)—stepping from one role to another seamlessly within the narrative of 1 Samuel. The overlap between his judicial and priestly responsibilities distinguishes him as the most unusual of the judges and lays the foundation for his role as prophet when he is called upon to designate Saul as God's choice as Israel's first king (1 Sam 8—9). Then there is a combination of judge and prophet when he is required on several occasions to hold Saul to a higher standard of behavior as God's anointed leader of the people (1 Sam 13 and 15). In that sense, he becomes the prototype for later prophets who also confront kings (see Elijah in 1 Kgs 18 and Isaiah in Isa 7).

Samuel's most important role, as it is portrayed in the biblical narrative, is as a figure who brings a measure of stability, judicial responsibility, and hope to the otherwise chaotic and disorganized period of the settlement. The Israelite tribes had benefited from similar leaders in the past (Moses and Joshua), but that type of leadership had been lacking for decades. The legacy of the temporary leadership provided by the judges is demonstrated once again in the inability of Samuel to pass his qualities on to his sons. This leads to the crisis that can only be dealt with by appointing a king. And even then, Samuel continues to function as the voice of caution in the face of great change, indicating to Saul that kings have their distinctive role that should not infringe on that of a priest (1 Sam 13) or a prophet.

27. What role do the Philistines play in the history of Israel?

The Philistines are a segment of a larger group known as the Sea Peoples, who invaded several areas of the ancient Near East around the year 1200 BCE. After destroying the Hittite kingdom in Anatolia and the seaport city of Ugarit in northern Syria, the Sea Peoples failed in their attempt to conquer Egypt and were repulsed by Pharaoh Ramesses III. At that point, with Egyptian control over Canaan effectively broken, the Philistines settled along the coastal plain of Canaan and eventually moved inland into the rolling plateau known as the Shephelah.

Since this disruption of the political situation in Canaan may have also facilitated the entrance of new peoples into the land, including the Israelites, competition for territory between these new settlers, the displaced population of some of the conquered Canaanite cities and the Philistines, took place. The Philistines were better organized militarily, technologically, and politically (1 Sam 13:19–22), and were able to carve out a sizable portion of the southern and central part of Canaan and to rule that area from five city-states (Gaza, Ashkelon, Ashdod, Ekron, and Gath). The Israelites and other new population elements settled in the less hospitable central highlands in loosely confederated villages. As one might expect, the dominance of the Philistines (see Judg 15:11) rankled their weaker rivals. The result was border skirmishes, disruption of trade by bandits, and the demonization of the Philistines in the biblical account as the "uncircumcised" (Judg 14:3; 1 Sam 14:6; 17:26). One reason Saul is chosen to lead the Israelite tribes as the war chief was to assist the tribes to compete militarily with the Philistines, and much of Saul's career is spent fighting them (1 Sam

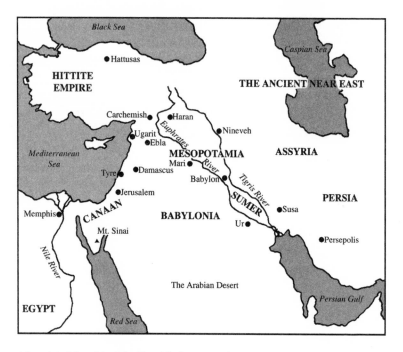

13—14; 28—29; 31). David also spends time as a mercenary "serving" the Philistine king Achish of Gath while learning their tactics and acquiring considerable wealth when his men raid Philistine villages and massacre their populations (1 Sam 27).

It is in part this cultural, economic, and political competition with the Philistines, and the desire on the part of the Israelites to expand beyond the hill country, that contribute to the establishment of the Israelite monarchy. Ultimately, the Philistines, like the Israelites, will become vassals of the Assyrians (post-800 BCE). Their cities and especially their strong olive oil industry are exploited by the Assyrians, and they are forced to submit, however unwillingly, to foreign rule (see the Ashdod Revolt of 711 BCE in Isa 20).

28. Who are the Amalekites, and what role do they play in Israelite history?

There is an interesting pattern of appearances by the Amalekites throughout Israelite history. Amalek is first noted in the Edomite genealogy of Esau, as the son of Eliphaz by a concubine (Gen 36:12), but all subsequent occurrences involve confrontations with the Israelite tribes. Military conflict begins in the Sinai wilderness, when the Amalekites dispute the use of their scare resources (water and grazing) by the Israelites, who have just exited Egypt. Their assault on the tribes, however, is repulsed when God intervenes in the guise of the Divine Warrior (Exod 17:8–13). Eternal enmity is then pronounced on the Amalekites: they are cursed by God to be "utterly blotted out," and the affirmation is made that there will be "war with Amalek from generation to generation" (Exod 17:14–16; curse reiterated in Deut 25:17–19).

When the twelve Israelite spies are sent into Canaan by Moses, they report that among the peoples currently in the land are the Amalekites, who inhabit the Negeb (Num 13:29). Lacking faith in the Divine Warrior's ability to overcome these peoples (Canaanites and Amalekites in Num 14:25), the Israelites are sent back into the wilderness rather than enjoy the "milk and honey" of the Promised Land. An aborted attempt to invade Canaan subsequently results in a defeat by the Amalekites and Canaanites and the Israelite flight to Hormah (Num 14:43–45). The Amalekites continue to be a thorn in Israel's side during the judges period, when they ally themselves with the Moabite king Eglon (Judg 3:13), raid Israelite fields and storage sheds along with the Midianites (Judg 6:3, 33), and oppose Gideon's efforts to throw off the oppression of these peoples (Judg 7:12).

During the early monarchy period, Samuel ordered Saul to "utterly destroy" the Amalekites, once again referencing "what they did in opposing the Israelites when they came up out of Egypt" (1 Sam 15:2–3). Saul's failure to complete this mission against the Amalekites results in Samuel's condemning statement that "the

LORD has torn the kingdom of Israel from you…and given it to a neighbor" (1 Sam 15:26–28). In this way, the Amalekites become the fulcrum for the emergence of David on the political scene and the basis for the disqualification of the Saulide dynasty from the kingship.

Furthermore, the enemy king of the Amalekites, Agag, who had been spared by Saul and then is executed by Samuel (1 Sam 15:20, 32–33), reappears far down the road in the form of Haman the Aggagite (Esth 3:1; 8:3). The use of the ethnic term *Aggagite* is a signal to the Israelite audience that this advisor to the Persian king is a remnant of their perennial enemy, the Amalekites, and a further indictment of Saul for failing to exterminate them when he had the chance. That same theme, casting shame on Saul and providing rich irony to the narrative, appears in the scene when Saul is surrounded by Philistines at the battle of Gilboa, and the only man who will slay the king to spare him the humiliation of being captured is an Amalekite (2 Sam 1:6–10). Putting closure to these pesky folk and certifying David's right to be king is a parallel story in which the future Israelite monarch rescues his household from Amalekite bandits at the very time that Saul was losing his final battle (2 Sam 30). Although the Amalekites are banished from the narrative at this point, there is one reference to their continued enmity as part of the peoples collectively named the "strong arm of Lot" (meaning the Transjordanian nations), who are allied with the Assyrians during the eighth century BCE against Israel (Ps 83:1–8).

29. Why do the people call on God and Samuel to give them a king? (1 Sam 8:1–15)

There are several factors that contribute to the people's desire for a king. The political chaos described in the Book of Judges that included oppression and military raids by neighboring peoples (Judg 3:12–14; 4:1–3; 6:1–7; 10:6–9) as well as civil war among the Israelite tribes (Judg 12:1–6; 20), kept the Israelites divided and weak. Although the shrine at Shiloh that housed the Ark of the

Covenant served as a pilgrimage point for the peoples of the hill country (1 Sam 1:3), the corrupt priesthood that served at the altar prevented it from becoming a rallying point for the tribes.

Even though Samuel was eventually able to unite the central portion of the hill country under his leadership and convince the tribes to accept his judicial authority as a circuit judge (1 Sam 7:5–17), the people still lacked a strong sense of national identity. It is also likely that the villages required more arable land to feed their growing populations and this made it necessary to expand ever-closer to Philistine territory. If they were going to be able to compete both militarily and economically with their stronger neighbors, then they needed a king "like other nations" (1 Sam 8:5). Only when they could exploit their natural resources, improve their technology and weaponry (see 1 Sam 13:19–22), travel freely to trade and to communicate with all regions of Canaan, engage in diplomatic relations with other nations, and draw upon the unifying factors of centralized government and a national religion could they hope to survive in this mixing pot of competing nations. The key was military parity with their neighbors and the creation of a national identity. Of course, the first kings of Israel will be little more than war chiefs since they will have to spend most of their reigns defending their territory and solidifying their political hold over the tribes. True centralized government with an effective bureaucracy, standing army, tax system, and long-range goals will have to wait till later generations.

30. How was Saul chosen as king, and what role did he play as a war chief?

The biblical narrative indicates that Saul was chosen by God to become Israel's "king" (meaning war chief) and that Samuel formalized this designation by anointing Saul with oil (1 Sam 9—10:1). As far as any particular qualifications are concerned, Saul is simply described as a tall young man, a good son, and a person who is willing to take advice in order to solve problems. These qualities are further enhanced after he is anointed when "God gave him another heart." He subsequently engages in a prophetic frenzy when he encounters a group of ecstatic prophets (1 Sam 10:9–13). Saul's real job, however, is to rally the Israelites around his leadership in war. Thus, even though he has received divine sanction, he will not be officially accepted as Israel's king until he has accomplished a significant military victory. That comes in the battle of Jabesh-gilead when Saul leads an allied army of tribes against the Ammonites and relieves the siege of the city. Thereafter, the victorious army travels south to Gilgal (site of Joshua's entrance into Canaan; Josh 4) where Saul's kingship is renewed and Samuel serves once again as God's spokesperson sanctioning this political office (1 Sam 11).

This campaign against the Ammonites is typical of Saul's career as war chief. He repeatedly rallies Israelite troops against an enemy, usually the Philistines (see 1 Sam 13:2–4), and has sufficient success to attract a cadre of warriors. Although he is able, like some of the judges, to "rescue Israel out of the hands of those who plundered them" (1 Sam 14:48), his reign is aptly summarized in 1 Samuel 14:52: "There was hard fighting against the Philistines all the days of Saul." He simply never had the time to be more than a military leader since the nation was always in crisis mode.

31. Why did Samuel challenge or condemn Saul's leadership on several occasions?

From the very beginning, Samuel was unhappy about the people's call for a king, and he made it clear that this was a rejection of God's ability to care for them and that there would be consequences that would include abuse of power and harsh treatment of the people by their rulers (see 1 Sam 8:11–18). These concerns set the stage for the confrontation between Samuel and Saul over the role of the king versus the role of priest and prophet. Like many prophets in later periods, Samuel was not about to cede his authority to Saul as a religious figure and spokesperson for God. Plus, a prophet who is an employee of the state is suspect because he serves two masters. Therefore, when Samuel relays instructions to Saul from God, the expectation is that they will be obeyed.

However, Saul has to deal with the realities of leadership during a time of war. When his soldiers begin to desert in the face of overwhelming odds, he feels he cannot wait more than the specified seven days on Samuel's return and instead makes a sacrifice and calls on God himself to lend his small army divine aid (1 Sam 13:8–12). Samuel has no patience for what he perceives as foolishness and disobedience to God's command (1 Sam 13:13–14). Clearly, the situation was desperate, and yet Samuel treats it as a test of Saul's faithfulness.

In a similar manner, Samuel instructs Saul to utterly destroy the Amalekites, killing every man, woman, and child and all of their livestock (1 Sam 15:3). The wastefulness of total warfare may have been behind Saul's decision, couched as the people's action, to spare King Agag, "the best of the sheep," and so on (15:9). When questioned about this, Saul assures the prophet that the animals will be sacrificed to God (15:21), but at that point Samuel voices the classic line that will become a sort of anthem used by prophets when confronting disobedient kings: "Surely, to obey is better than sacrifice" (15:22). Ultimately, Samuel's challenges and condemnations of Saul hinge on a very strict interpretation of what is acceptable to God regardless of military or political realities or expediencies. This is also the tone of the Deuteronomistic history that judges kings by their faithfulness and fidelity to God rather than their political acumen. In addition, the reality here is that Saul's dynasty is supplanted by David's, and it is the Davidic scribal community that composes the history of this period. It is in their interests to make a case against Saul; his disputes with Samuel serve that purpose, while at the same time establishing the role of the prophet as the champion of God's command.

32. How does David become Saul's political rival?

Newly established chiefdoms like ancient Israel are difficult to hold together because they are dependent on the success of the war chief and on his ability to maintain strong political ties with the tribal leaders. Saul's reign had only mixed success in fighting the Philistines and other neighboring peoples. His support among the tribes began to erode as the situation became more desperate, and as Saul's mental state was perceived to be unstable (perhaps best evidenced by his massacre of the priests at Nob; 1 Sam 22:6–19). It is therefore not surprising that a legitimate political rival would emerge to challenge the king and his family's right to the throne.

The story of how David rose to that position is sometimes referred to as the "apology of David," that is, a sympathetic and politically biased version of events created by his supporters as a way of demonstrating his right to usurp the throne of a failed ruler. The chart below demonstrates the major steps that lead David from obscurity as a simple shepherd boy to a member of the royal family and ultimately to become a legitimate political rival to King Saul:

1 Sam 16:1–13 Samuel is instructed by God to go to Bethlehem to meet with Jesse and to identify the next "LORD's anointed" from among his sons. David is chosen.

1 Sam 16:14–23 To ease Saul's mental distress, David is dispatched to the palace to play the harp and eventually joins Saul's service as his armor-bearer.

1 Sam 17 David accepts Goliath's challenge, kills the giant Philistine, gives heart to the Israelites to defeat the Philistines, and is able to claim a royal daughter.

1 Sam 18:1–7 David wins over Saul's son Jonathan as a friend (see also 1 Sam 20) and gains the acclaim of the people with his military exploits with a chant extolling his killing of "ten thousands" (18:7).

1 Sam 18:17–30 David marries Saul's daughter Michal after presenting a bride price of 200 Philistine foreskins. He continues to have military success over Philistines.

1 Sam 21:1–9 Forced to flee from Saul's jealous wrath (1 Sam 19:8–17), David forms an outlaw band and obtains the sword of Goliath from the priests at Nob.

1 Sam 24 While Saul seeks to kill David, David spares Saul's life rather than harm the "LORD's anointed" (see 1 Sam 26 for another example of this policy decision).

1 Sam 25 David creates a social and political network through multiple marriages.

1 Sam 27 While serving as a mercenary chief for the Philistine king Achish, David raids Philistine villages, learns Philistine tactics, and shares his loot with the elders of Judah to gain their support (see 1 Sam 30:26–31).

33. How does David take advantage of his position as an outlaw?

When David is forced to flee Saul's palace rather than face the king's murderous wrath (1 Sam 19:8–17), he is joined by his brothers, as well as other members of his father's household, at the Cave of Adullam in the Shephelah region. In addition, in much the same way as they did for the people of Robin Hood's time in medieval England, "Everyone who was in distress...in debt...and discontented gathered to him" as their captain (1 Sam 22:1–2). After finding sanctuary for his parents with the king of Moab (1 Sam 22:3–4), David went back into the Judean wilderness and the sparsely uninhabited areas of the hill country (Forest of Hereth; 1 Sam 22:5). Playing off the disaffection caused by Saul's policies and his failure to eliminate the Philistine threat, David uses his position as an "outsider" to gain support and to erode the political loyalties of the tribal elders.

The contrast between an old, distrustful king and his young rival is made crystal clear in two events shortly after David is outlawed. After David went to the priestly city of Nob to obtain food for his men and the sword of Goliath (1 Sam 21:1–9; a visible symbol of David's hero status), Saul irrationally orders a massacre of the priests. Only Abiathar escapes and he quickly joins David's band (a sort of Friar Tuck figure), demonstrating the shift of priestly commitment from Saul to David (1 Sam 22:6–23). In a second instance, David, with God's assurance of success, rescues the city of Keilah (six miles northwest of Hebron in the eastern Shephelah) from Philistine incursions (1 Sam 23:1–5). Instead of rejoicing that David had struck a blow against the Philistines, Saul sees this as an opportunity to trap David within a walled city and as a result David is forced once again to flee (1 Sam 23:7–14). Despite having to abandon Keilah, David has made the point that he is acting at God's command rather than to harm his rival.

When it becomes clear that Saul will not give up his search for the young outlaw, David steps away from Israelite territory and approaches Achish, the Philistine king of Gath, offering his services as a mercenary chief. Although this could be perceived as traitorous behavior, the narrative turns it into a plus by noting how David's men raid Philistine villages, leaving no survivors to tell the tale. He acquires so much loot that he cannot only share it with Achish and please his master (1 Sam 27), but also with the Judean elders, solidifying their support (1 Sam 30:26–31). David would also learn Philistine military tactics and, perhaps, some new weapons technology that eventually could be used to help the Israelites in battle. Finally, the stories of how David spares Saul's life (1 Sam 24 and 26) again contrast the two, one merciful and faithful to God and the other revengeful and cut off from contact with God, the priests, and the prophets (1 Sam 28:3–5).

34. What is the case against Saul's dynasty that allows David to become king?

As the first "king" of Israel, Saul faced the dual dilemma of trying to defend the tribal territories from outside enemies and trying to hold his coalition of tribes together during the years of continuous fighting. It is not surprising that he was criticized because much of what he tried to do was new and there would have been many looking for an opportunity to remove him in favor of their own champion.

However, the editors that produced the "apology of David," which functions as the case against Saul's dynasty and the case for David's taking the throne, were not entirely free to rewrite the traditions about Saul's reign, and there are clearly some well-known events that they could not change. This helps to explain why there are some very positive statements made about Saul's efforts as war chief that remain in the text (1 Sam 14:47–52). However, the bulk of the narrative makes a very strong case to disqualify Saul and his family from the kingship. The chart below supplies the major charges and political polemics used against Saul.

---

1 Sam 10:17–27 When Samuel assembled the people at Mizpah and cast lots for a king, Saul was chosen, but he was discovered hiding with the baggage (10:22), causing some men to despise him (10:27).

1 Sam 11:5–7 The act of courage and dedication in which Saul sacrifices his oxen, cuts up their bodies, and uses these pieces to rally the tribes to save Jabesh-gilead is parodied in the horrendous act of the Levite who cuts his concubine into twelve pieces after she is raped to death in Gibeah (Saul's hometown) to rally the tribes to punish the tribe of Benjamin (Saul's tribe; Judg 19:27–30).

1 Sam 13:8–14 Saul makes a burnt offering without waiting for Samuel to return. The prophet condemns the king and tells him God will choose another to rule because of this failure to keep the Lord's command.

1 Sam 14 Saul's ill-considered oath that forbids his men to eat during battle condemns his son Jonathan. When the army refuses to turn the young man over for execution, Saul loses face and a large measure of his authority.

1 Sam 15 Samuel relays God's command to carry out a *herem* against the Amalekites. Although victorious, he preserves the best animals and King Agag for sacrifice and a public show of his power. Samuel decries this failure to obey God's command and predicts that the kingdom will be torn away from Saul and that God would choose a more faithful servant to be king.

1 Sam 16:14–23 Saul is portrayed as a mentally unstable ruler.

1 Sam 18:6–16 David, who had defeated the Philistine champion Goliath, is hailed as a warrior ten times more successful than Saul. This opens a breach between the two that leads to Saul attempting to kill David and driving him into outlawry.

1 Sam 22:6–19 A jealous and unstable Saul orders the massacre of the priests at Nob for aiding his rival David.

1 Sam 28:3–25 Cut off from any communication with God, Saul breaks his own command and consults a witch at Endor. Samuel's spirit then predicts the death of the king and his sons at the battle of Gilboa.

PART FOUR
United Monarchy

35. What is the literary structure and plot of the Second Book of Samuel?

The Second Book of Samuel is filled with political plots and counterplots. The story begins with the transition of power after the death of Saul (2 Sam 1). Despite David's evident popularity, one son of Saul, Ishbaal, lives and claims the kingship, although he must do so from Transjordanian exile in Mahanaim. David therefore establishes himself in Hebron for the next seven years during which there are raids and skirmishes between his men, led by his cousin Joab, and Ishbaal's warriors, led by Saul's former general Abner (2 Sam 2). Intrigue and a desire for power lead to Abner's and Ishbaal's deaths, and this opens the door for David to be proclaimed king by all of the tribal elders (2 Sam 3—5). David then moves swiftly to consolidate his power and to establish national symbols and a centralized seat of government by capturing Jerusalem, bringing the Ark of the Covenant to his new capital city, and placing Joab in charge of a standing army (2 Sam 6—10). With the monarchy firmly in place and bolstered by the proclamation of the "everlasting covenant" between God and the Davidic dynasty (1 Sam 7), the narrative then turns to the issue of succession and the difficulties caused by the rivalries among David's sons. The narrative provides a theological spark for these internal conflicts when the prophet Nathan condemns David for his adultery with Bathsheba (2 Sam 11—12).

However, the contest between Amnon and Absalom for the right to be the heir (2 Sam 13—14), and then the contest between David and Absalom that leads David to temporarily flee his capital (2 Sam 15—19), are typical of newly established kingdoms. They exemplify the difficulties of keeping peace within a royal household and with tribes whose natural tendency is to ignore or pull away from the central government whenever possible (see Sheba's Revolt in 2 Sam 20). The book ends with David's ill-conceived census, God's punishment, and the purchase of the threshing floor of Araunah that will eventually serve as the site of Solomon's Temple (2 Sam 24).

36. Why is it significant that David reigned first in Hebron?

One rule of thumb in reading the biblical narratives is to ask the question, "Why did this event occur in this particular place?" In this case, Hebron has a past association with the ancestral traditions. It is the town where Abraham purchased the cave of Machpelah to serve as a burial site for his wife (Gen 23), and it was subsequently used as the tomb for all of the ancestors and their households. Hebron is centrally located in the tribal territory of Judah, David's tribe, making it a logical political center for his role as tribal chief. Since he could not immediately obtain the political allegiance of the other tribal leaders after the death of Saul, he had to continue to build his political network in his bid for king of Israel. It made sense that he would draw upon authoritative traditions of the past and make use of the loyalties of his own tribe during the seven years—an interesting number given its use in the creation story (Gen 1:1—2:4a) and in the Jacob narratives (Gen 29:18, 30)—he ruled in Hebron.

Having been anointed by the people of Judah as their "king" (2 Sam 2:4), David's administrative presence in Hebron gives him a political edge over his rival Ishbaal, who must reign over Israel from the Transjordanian province of Gilead and the city of Mahanaim on the Jabbock River (2 Sam 2:8–10). In this case, geography is everything. David rules Judah from within the Promised Land and Ishbaal claims to rule Israel from outside of Canaan (compare this to Abram's separation from Lot, who chose to move to the area of Sodom in Transjordan and was disqualified as an heir of the covenant; Gen 13:8–13).

37. What role does Joab play in the cycle of stories about David?

During the period of the early monarchy, it is quite common for both Saul and David to make use of members of their extended family in their administration. Thus Joab, David's first cousin, plays a very prominent role throughout David's career, principally as a military leader. Always the more pragmatic of the two when it comes to the interests of the state, Joab often takes matters into his own hands to do what he thinks is best, either to protect David or to preserve the viability of the royal house. David will not always thank his cousin for these actions, and in fact he relieves him of his duties on several occasions. However, there is no officer more loyal to David and the king repeatedly finds himself in a position in which he must restore Joab to command. The chart below outlines the up-and-down cycle of Joab's career in David's service.

2 Sam 2:12–32 During David's seven-year reign in Hebron, Joab commands his forces that skirmish on their border with Ishbaal's men, led by Abner.

2 Sam 3:22–39 When Abner attempts to defect to David's side, Joab argues against this and then kills Abner. David disavows this act that could affect his attempt to unite the tribes and forces Joab to mourn for Abner publicly.

2 Sam 10:7–14 Joab is appointed to lead the army (2 Sam 8:16) and defeats the Ammonite-Aramean coalition. In subsequent campaigns, "David stayed in Jerusalem" rather than leading the army himself (2 Sam 11:1).

2 Sam 11 When David commits adultery with Bathsheba, the wife of Uriah the Hittite, he orders Joab to place Uriah in the front lines so he will be killed (11:14–25).

2 Sam 12:26–31 After besieging the Ammonite capital of Rabbah and taking its outer defenses, Joab calls on David to command the final step in taking the city so that the king could claim the victory and the spoil.

2 Sam 14:1–24 When the internal fighting between Amnon and Absalom results in Amnon's death and Absalom's exile, Joab stages a scene for David in which the "wise woman" of Tekoa petitions the king to spare her son. David recognizes this as Joab's ploy to preserve the line of succession and allows Joab to bring Absalom back to the royal court.

2 Sam 14:25–33 Joab serves as a go-between to reconcile David and Absalom.

2 Sam 18—19:15 In order to retake Jerusalem from Absalom's forces, a pitched battle is fought in the forest of Ephraim. David had cautioned Joab to "deal gently" with Absalom (18:5), but Joab kills Absalom and buries his body (18:14–18). David goes into mourning for his son. Joab has to shock the king into thanking the army for restoring his kingdom, but David then gives the command of the army to Amasa (19:13).

2 Sam 20:4–23 During Sheba's revolt, Amasa delays taking action so Joab visits the army camp, assassinates him (20:8–10), and then leads the army against the rebel. Action ends with the death of the rebels at Abel Bethmaacah and Joab's restoration as commander of the king's forces.

The final chapter in this drama of David and Joab occurs during the struggle over the succession when Joab favors David's son Adonijah over Solomon (1 Kgs 1:7). In his instructions to Solomon, David warns his successor of Joab's plots and murders, and he recommends that the new king "not let his [Joab's] gray head go down to Sheol [the underworld] in peace" (1 Kgs 2:5–6). Clearly, in the world of bloody politics that characterized the court of David, a tool such as Joab eventually became too dangerous to leave in place to cause further mischief.

38. Why does David choose Jerusalem as his new capital city and then bring the Ark there? (2 Sam 5—6)

Although David ruled for seven years in Hebron, he could not continue to use that city because it was located too far south and was tied too firmly to the tribe of Judah. He needed a capital city that was more centrally located and thus enabled him to communicate more quickly with the various tribal areas. It was also important that the site be one that was easily defended and, even more importantly, that it be politically neutral. Jerusalem filled these specifications quite well. Its defenses had not been breached during the settlement period, and it continued to be inhabited by the Jebusites (Josh 15:63; Judg 1:21).

In addition, Jerusalem's value as a regional center had a history going back to at least the Amarna period (fourteenth century BCE), when it was the seat of an Egyptian-appointed governor. In fact, it is quite likely that David did not kill the people of Jebus/Jerusalem when he took and then expanded the city (2 Sam 5:6–10). He needed people with skills who could step in and help him run his newly established kingdom. David also needed a national symbol to draw the focus of the tribes to Jerusalem. The most effective symbol that he could command was the Ark of the Covenant. This holy object, the repository for the tablets of the Law (Exod 25:16; Deut 10:1–5), had been kept in the tent of meeting throughout the Exodus and wilderness period. When Joshua brought the Israelites into Canaan, the Ark led the way in crossing the Jordan River (Josh 3). It represented God's presence when it was carried into battle (Josh 6:1–16). However, the power of the Ark was intimately tied to respect for God, and when Eli's corrupt sons carried it into battle against the Philistines, God allowed the Ark to be captured (1 Sam 4:6–11).

When it was restored to the Israelites, there were no qualified Levites available to minister to the Ark and therefore it was stored away throughout Saul's reign in the small village of Kiriath-jearim

(1 Sam 6—7:2). David chose to bring the Ark back into public view as a way to tie his dynasty to the covenant promise and to bolster his claims of leadership over all the tribes. However, he was reminded of the Ark's power when he initially failed to transport it properly at the cost of a man's life (2 Sam 6:1–11). Recognizing his error, David made an offering and after a suitable period brought the Ark with great fanfare to Jerusalem. His entrance into the city, dancing and celebrating nearly naked before the Ark (2 Sam 6:14–15), may be a further sign of his submission to Yahweh, but it clearly pleased the people, providing an impression of a king willing to humble himself and join in their public celebration. Once the Ark was installed within the city, it ceases to stir (see 2 Sam 15:24–26) and becomes a permanent fixture tied eventually to Solomon's Temple (1 Kgs 6:19) and ever after to the Davidic dynasty.

39. Did David really have an "empire"?

The biblical account describes a series of wars in which David defeats the rulers of the Transjordanian kingdoms of Edom, Moab, and Ammon, as well as the Syrian kingdoms of Zobah and Hamath (2 Sam 8:1–14; 10:6–19). In some cases David is aided by alliances with former vassal states of the Syrians, who wished either to take revenge on the Syrians or to take advantage of the conflict in order to gain territory and loot (2 Sam 8:9–10). Unfortunately, we do not have records from these other nations to corroborate the biblical narrative. The archaeological record is also inconclusive because ancient battles are difficult to trace, and much of the evidence of monumental construction (fortified cities gates and walls) from the eleventh century BCE has been destroyed or reused by later builders.

As a result, in order to answer this question, it is necessary to imagine a period in which there are a number of small kingdoms, some like David's, attempting to consolidate their power and protect their borders. It is not beyond the realm of possibility that David did make diplomatic contact with these neighboring peoples and in some cases engaged in armed conflict to protect or expand his interests. However, the nation of Israel is only beginning to establish a sense of national identity at this point and would not have the resources in men or material to engage in sustained conflicts. It is therefore more likely that David would have concentrated his efforts on protecting his borders within Canaan, while taking account against any armed incursion that may have attempted to test his resolve or his defenses. To answer the question then, the "empire" ascribed to David in the account in 2 Samuel is therefore unlikely. The most that could be hoped for in David's time was to hold together the tribal territories, and even this was sometimes in question (see Sheba's Revolt in 2 Sam 20).

40. What is the significance of the "everlasting covenant"? (2 Sam 7:8–17)

The establishment of the "everlasting covenant" with the house of David occurs in the context of David's desire to build a "house" (i.e., a temple) to house the Ark of the Covenant, which will also be a further symbol of David's and the new Israelite nation's power. The intermediary in this drama is the prophet Nathan, who initially states that God has sanctioned the construction of a temple and then returns to David to say that God does not desire "a house of cedar" (2 Sam 7:4–7). Instead, God extends the metaphor of a house to the idea of a royal dynasty and makes a divine pledge to David that "your house and your kingdom shall be made sure forever.... Your throne shall be established forever" (2 Sam 7:16). David accepts this gracious offer of "divine-right rule" for his royal house in a prayer to God that reiterates God's promise and that pledges to magnify God's name forever with the creedal statement that "the LORD of hosts is God over Israel" (2 Sam 7:18–29).

What is particularly significant about this dynastic covenant is the political stability that it will provide to David's successors. The line of succession is established from father to son (7:12) and only two kings in four hundred years will be assassinated, a record that many other kingdoms could envy and never claim. Furthermore, any attempt to rebel against a Davidic ruler, based on his failure to be just or to be in all ways honorable, is set aside by God's statement that punishment may occur "with blows inflicted by human beings," but the kingdom and the dynasty will persist (2 Sam 7:14–16).

41. Was David an effective administrator and military leader?

The account of David's reign provides much more information on his abilities as a military leader than as an administrator. In fact, one short passage summarizes his administration as consisting of Joab as his army chief, a recorder, two high priests, a secretary, and a commander of his royal guard (2 Sam 8:15–18). This suggests a very small bureaucracy for a fledging state that was primarily concerned with maintaining its existence amid a sea of hostile neighboring peoples. There are also indications in the text that David at times had to be nudged into making decisions (Joab's use of the wise woman of Tekoa in 2 Sam 14:1–24), and there were instances when David could be accused of failing to appoint judges or to hear the cases of the people (2 Sam 15:2–6).

David's military record is much better. For much of his life he effectively led men into battle and employed military strategies that produced victories on the battlefield. Like other military leaders of his time, David was a pragmatist. He was willing to take no prisoners when it was necessary to maintain secrecy (1 Sam 27:8–12), and to employ psychological tactics by killing prisoners of war to frighten enemies into submission (2 Sam 8:2). With the exception of his appointment of Amasa as his general (2 Sam 20:4–5), David made good use of his military commanders when it became too dangerous for him to hazard his own person in battle (2 Sam 18:3–4).

42. Why does Nathan tell David the parable of the ewe lamb? (2 Sam 12:1–15)

As Samuel warned the people when they cried out for the establishment of the monarchy, kings will at times abuse their power and will oppress the people they are called upon to rule (1 Sam 8:11–18). David fulfills this prediction when he commits adultery with Bathsheba and then has her husband Uriah killed by sending him to the front lines in battle (2 Sam 11). Even though it appears that David has escaped punishment for this capital offense (Lev 18:19–20; Deut 22:22), it is the role of the prophet Nathan to remind David that the king is not above the law. Rather than accusing the king publicly, since there were no human witnesses, the prophet goes to David and poses a case to the king in the form of a juridical parable.

This procedure falls within David's jurisdiction as chief judicial officer in the kingdom. The rather transparent story of a rich man abusing a poor man by confiscating the poor man's ewe lamb is apparently beyond David's present ability to discern. Therefore, instead of seeing himself in the role of the rich man, David condemns the man to pay a fourfold fine and declares that the man "deserves to die...because he had no pity" (2 Sam 12:1–6). Having unwittingly cast judgment on himself, David is now denounced by Nathan who announces, "You are the man!" (12:7). Rather than given a fine or the death penalty, however, David is confronted with the long-term sentence, "The sword shall never depart from your house" (12:10), plus God's intent to "raise up trouble against you from within your house" (12:11). In addition, the child born of Bathsheba, physical evidence of David's sin, will die (12:14). The result of this confrontation, which does not result in the loss of the kingship by David or his successors, is nevertheless a prolonged and painful period in which David's sons fight over the right to become his heir. Nathan's parable not only provides a prologue to these violent episodes, but also provides a precedent for other prophets who will call kings to justice (see Ahab and Elijah in 1 Kgs 21).

43. What is the succession narrative, and what is its significance?

For there to be an orderly succession from one king to another in a hereditary monarchy, some process needs to be developed to determine who is to be the rightful heir. What complicates this is the number of potential heirs produced by a king with many wives, like David. Of course, David could have designated which of his sons would succeed him, but apparently that did not happen. Instead, each of the sons engages in plots to weaken the other principal claimants or forms a faction of supporters to bolster his right to the kingship. The succession narrative contained in the latter half of 2 Samuel and the beginning chapters of 1 Kings present a soap-opera narrative involving rape, murder, usurpation of power, civil war, and the purging of failed claimants and their supporters.

While this is an extremely messy process and one that often casts David as an oblivious father or a distracted ruler, the succession narrative may well retain both historical information as well as a good measure of the struggles that tend to take place in newly formed royal courts. It is also possible that the difficulties described in this narrative are intended to serve as an argument for future kings to be more diligent in designating their successor (note that Solomon's successor Rehoboam has no such struggle to cope with; 1 Kgs 11:41–43). The chart below provides a basic summary of these events:

2 Sam 13:1–22 Amnon convinces David to send Absalom's sister Tamar to him to cook his meals. He then rapes her and sends her back to Absalom. The inability to protect his sister weakens Absalom's claim to the heirship.

2 Sam 13:23–39 Two years later Absalom arranges the murder of Amnon and is forced to go into exile, leaving the nation without a likely successor.

2 Sam 15—16 After Joab engineers Absalom's return to court (2 Sam 14), Absalom creates a body of supporters and undermines David by claiming his father is incompetent (15:1–12). When Absalom is proclaimed king in Hebron, David is forced to flee Jerusalem from the oncoming army of the usurper, although the king does leave behind the seeds of restoration (Hushai, the double agent).

> **2 Sam 18—20** Even though Absalom's army is eventually defeated and he is killed by Joab, David's apparent weakness as king sparks a rebellion of the northern tribes led by Sheba (2 Sam 20), which Joab is forced to suppress.
>
> **1 Kgs 1—2** Once David becomes too old to rule, his sons Adonijah and Solomon vie for the throne with the latter winning the day with the help of Nathan and his mother Bathsheba. Subsequently, Adonijah's major supporters are killed (Joab) or exiled (Abiathar). Eventually, Adonijah is also executed.

44. What is the literary structure and plot of the First Book of Kings?

The First Book of Kings is filled with the abridged and edited royal annals of the kings of Israel and Judah. Compiled and edited by the Deuteronomistic Historian at the end of the monarchy period, this material is shaped to highlight the importance of Jerusalem and its Temple, the Davidic monarchy, and the political and religious failures of the kings of the Northern Kingdom of Israel. The first eleven chapters involve—

Solomon's coming to the throne (1 Kgs 1–2)
his portrayal as a wise king and a skilled administrator
(1 Kgs 3—4; 9:15—10)
the construction and dedication of the Jerusalem Temple to
Yahweh (1 Kgs 5—9:14)
Solomon's errors (apostasy when he builds shrines to the
gods of his many wives) and growing political opposition
(1 Kgs 11)

Following Solomon's death, the book turns to the events leading to the division of the kingdom (1 Kgs 12:1–24), and then the Deuteronomistic Historian lays out the criteria upon which all future kings of these nations will be judged: Jeroboam's sin (1 Kgs

12:25–33; see question 51). The collected annals of the kings of Israel reveal a nation characterized by political instability, assassinations, conflict with Judah and other nations, and continued violations of the covenant (1 Kgs 13—16). Most of the kings of Israel receive little attention from the editors, but King Ahab and his wife Jezebel have extended coverage in order to showcase how corrupt and oppressive a monarch could be (1 Kgs 17—21). These episodes also introduce the prophet Elijah as the champion of Yahweh and the model for later prophets who will condemn social injustice and covenant violation. The final chapter contains a confrontation between Ahab and the prophet Micaiah and provides insights on court prophets, dreams, and military tactics (1 Kgs 22).

45. How does Solomon become David's successor? (1 Kgs 1—2)

Like his father David, who was the youngest of Jesse's sons, Solomon will come to power in place of his older brother Adonijah. The elements in the story that make this possible are the backing of the prophet Nathan and his mother Bathsheba, the ill-considered actions of Adonijah publicly proclaiming he assumed he would become king (1 Kgs 1:5–7, 9), and David's apparent lack of mental acuity. Both Adonijah and Solomon had formed political factions led by important members of David's court.

Joab and the priest Abiathar favored Adonijah while Solomon's party included the priest Zadok, the prophet Nathan, and Benaiah, the commander of the palace guard (1:8). Seeing Adonijah becoming more bold in asserting his rights to the throne, Nathan and Bathsheba conspire to convince David that he had previously sworn that "Solomon shall succeed me as king" (1:11–27). Angry at Adonijah's staging of a feast and taking on the airs of a king, David swears that Solomon will be his heir (1:28–31). This sets in motion a quick sequence of events in which Solomon is escorted to Gihon where he is anointed king by Zadok and Nathan, and a trumpeting fanfare and shout proclaims, "Long live King Solomon" (1:32–40). Startled by the sound, Adonijah discovers he has been outmaneuvered. His dinner guests and political allies scatter, and Adonijah has no choice but to do obeisance to the new king (1:41–53). Following these events and at the suggestion of a now lucid David, Joab is executed and Abiathar is exiled. When Adonijah shows that he is a danger, Adonijah is also executed (1 Kgs 2). With the political field cleared, "the kingdom was established in the hand of Solomon" (2:46).

46. How does Solomon earn the title "wise king"? (1 Kgs 3; 4:29–34; 9:15–28; 10)

There is a real attempt on the part of the biblical editors to paint a picture of peace and prosperity during the time of King Solomon. One part of this picture is the creation of a positive persona for Solomon as a "wise king." They may have felt this was necessary given the mental lapses and political infighting that took place in the latter part of David's reign. Solomon's wisdom label is firmly established in the story of his dream theophany at Gibeon in which God offers the king at the beginning of his reign the opportunity to ask for a gift.

Solomon requests that God grant him "an understanding mind to govern your people" (1 Kgs 3:3–10). Such a selfless request pleases God and Solomon then is granted wisdom as well as "riches and honor" throughout his reign (3:10–14). With this as a preface, there are several subsequent scenes in which the king displays how his God-given wisdom contributes to the establishment of justice for his people and insures the growing wealth and prosperity for the nation:

1 Kgs 3:16–28 Using a psychological ploy, Solomon discerns which of two prostitutes is the true mother of a child. Compare this judicial audience for the lowliest of subjects to David's failure to hear cases or appoint judges (2 Sam 15:2–6).

1 Kgs 4:29–34 A summary statement of Solomon's remarkable wisdom describes him as the author of thousands of

proverbs, an authority on all aspects of nature, and a human wonder that brought people from all nations to hear him speak.

1 Kgs 9:15–28 Coupled with his reorganization of the bureaucracy and the tribal territories (1 Kgs 4:1–28), this passage recounts Solomon's judicious fortification of Israel's borders, formation of labor gangs for public projects, his regular sacrificial offerings to God, and his many commercial activities.

1 Kgs 10 Solomon's fame and abilities as a sage are tested and confirmed by the Queen of Sheba. Many others brought him rich presents and were quick to join his far-flung commercial enterprises in many lands.

Of course, no human king is perfect in his judgment, and ultimately Solomon will fail to maintain his required allegiance to God. His governmental reorganization and the cultural influences introduced by his many foreign wives will spark opposition from within his administration, from the tribal leaders, and from neighboring countries (1 Kgs 11).

47. What products and natural resources contributed to Israel's economy?

Ancient Israel was a small country with limited natural resources and no natural harbors. However, it had sufficient arable farmland to produce surpluses of wheat and barley, as well as abundant sheep, goats, and cattle. Its hillsides and Mediterranean climate made it an ideal location for vineyards and olive groves. Thus, a basic inventory of the natural resources, manufactured goods, and agricultural products typical of the internal economy in the tenth century BCE would include bitumen, potash and phosphates from the Dead Sea area (Gen 14:10), pottery, textiles, wine, olive oil, and various cereal grains.

The description of the provisions supplied to Solomon's royal court adds further detail, including cattle, sheep, and wild game for his table (1 Kgs 4:22–23). With the establishment of the monarchy and especially in Solomon's time when a peacetime economy was launched, more attention was given to the creation of trade links with other nations. In particular, the combination of an alliance between Solomon and Hiram of the Phoenician kingdom of Tyre, and the construction of a fleet of ships, allowed for a wide-ranging policy of trade with areas in Africa and Arabia (9:26–28). Connections were also made with Syrian and "Hittite" (northern Mesopotamian and Anatolian) areas that were interested in acquiring large numbers of horses (10:29). A large variety of manufactured and luxury goods then began to flow into Israel, including cedar logs for the Temple and the palaces in Jerusalem (9:11), spices and precious stones (10:10–12), as well as apes, ivory, and peacocks from Africa (10:22).

48. How do Ahijah's designation of Jeroboam and Rehoboam's lack of diplomacy combine to create a division in the kingdom? (1 Kgs 11:29—12:19)

In order to explain the division of the kingdom following Solomon's reign, the biblical account provides two distinct narratives. The first is predicated on God's displeasure over Solomon's apostasy when he constructed shrines for his foreign wives' gods (1 Kgs 11:1–13). In response to God's anger over this infidelity, internal and external political adversaries are "raised up" that trouble Solomon's reign (11:14–25). Then, to deal with issues in the next generation, God instructs the prophet Ahijah to designate an Israelite leader who would be given rule over ten tribes (11:31–39). Ahijah, in much the same manner that Samuel designated David (1 Sam 16:1–13), secretly confronts Jeroboam ben Nebat, a man unrelated to the royal house, on the road away from Jerusalem. He presents him with the opportunity to rule the northern tribes if he proves faithful to Yahweh (11:37–38). An interesting piece of symbolism is part of this offer: The prophet takes hold of Jeroboam's robe, tears it into twelve pieces, and then presents him with ten, thereby demonstrating in this way that Jeroboam will have charge of these ten tribes (11:29–32).

Although Solomon will force Jeroboam into exile in Egypt for the remainder of his reign (11:40), he returns at the critical moment when the tribal elders call Solomon's son and successor Rehoboam to a conference at Shechem (12:1–5). This is a crucial moment in Israelite history. The tribes ask for more local autonomy and fewer demands on their resources by the central government. Rehoboam, who listens only to his younger, less-experienced advisers, has no intention of negotiating with the elders. Instead, he attempts to frighten them into submission to his rule by boasting that "I will add to your yoke" and "I will discipline you with scorpions" (12:14). The harshness of his tone and his blustering self-assurance quickly turns the conference into a shambles and drives the tribal elders to abandon the "house of David." It is a simple matter to turn instead to Jeroboam as their ruler because he had already been chosen by God (12:16–20). As a result, only the tribe of Judah remains loyal to Rehoboam. Although he assembled an army to reclaim the lost territory, Rehoboam is commanded by the prophet Shemaiah to abandon his plans since it is God's will that he accept the secession of the northern tribes (12:21–24). The result of these events is that the hereditary monarchy established by David continues to rule Judah from Jerusalem, while the northern tribes will have a less stable political arrangement characterized by short-lived dynasties and repeated assassinations.

PART FIVE

Divided Monarchy

49. What role did Ammon, Moab, and Edom play in Israel's history?

Ammon, Moab, and Edom are the three Transjordanian kingdoms that alternated throughout Israelite history as allies, vassals, and enemies. None of these petty kingdoms were strong enough to carve out their own miniempire, but they were a key to Israel's control or use of natural resources and trade routes in Transjordan, and thus they are continually woven into the narrative (see Judg 3:13; 10:6–18; 1 Sam 10:27—11:11; 2 Sam 10:1–19) and in the prophetic literature (Jer 25:17–26; Ezek 21:28–32; Zeph 2:8–9). Their traditional origin goes back to Abraham and his extensive household.

Lot was Abraham's nephew and he traveled with him to Canaan (Gen 12:4–5). When their flocks grew too large to be grazed in a single area, Lot and Abraham separated and Lot chose to settle in Transjordan in the city of Sodom (Gen 13:5–13). After Sodom was destroyed, Lot's daughters got their father drunk so that he would impregnate them, and the result of these incestuous relations was the birth of Ammon and Moab (Gen 19:30–38). Edom is the domain of Jacob's brother Esau, who is supplanted as heir of the covenant (Gen 36:1–14). The shameful origin ascribed to Ammon and Moab often serves as political propaganda justifying Israel's many skirmishes with these nations. For example, Moab is a vassal of the kingdom of Israel during Omri's reign in the mid-ninth century BCE. Their subsequent rebellion is described in both 2 Kings 3 as well as in the Moabite inscription of King Mesha (Matthews and Benjamin, *Old Testament Parallels*, 167–69). Edom, while eventually more closely related to the covenantal community, is vilified as an enemy in David's time (2 Sam 8:13–14) and during the reigns of later kings, who wished to control the southern Transjordan and its links to the Gulf of Aqaba (2 Kgs 14:1–10). Even greater enmity is created when Edom chose to raid Israelite territory (Amos

1:11–12) and later allied themselves with the Babylonians and assist in the conquest of Judah (Ps 137:7; Oba 1—8).

50. How do Judah and Israel differ, and how will this affect their history?

The first way to answer this question is to look at the geography and natural resources of these two small nations. Judah consists of far less territory and less arable land to support agricultural activity. It is dominated by the southern portion of the central hill country and is cut off from the Mediterranean coast by the Philistine city-states. Its southern reaches include the Judean wilderness and the northern Negeb, neither of which can sustain large urban centers or a substantial population. In fact, other than the cities of Jerusalem, Lachish, Hebron, and Beer-sheba, Judah is characterized by small farming villages of 100 to 200 people, like Tekoa. This stands in contrast to the Northern Kingdom of Israel that boasts several cities (Bethel, Shiloh, Shechem, Gibeon, Samaria, Megiddo, and Hazor). The Via Maris links Israel with Syria and Phoenicia to the north and east and provides access for both commercial and military expeditions. The climate in Israel is characterized by higher annual rainfall amounts than in Judah, and there are much larger areas that can be devoted to intensive agricultural and pastoral use. In particular, surpluses of wheat, wine, olive oil, and cattle formed the basis for trade with other countries. Israel's larger population also allows it to engage in more extensive public works (roads, bridges, fortified cities), military enterprises that brought much of Transjordan under their control, decades of warfare with the Syrians, and wide-ranging commercial activity.

In nearly every way Israel is a much more desirable area than Judah when examined from the viewpoint of topography and economic potential. However, Judah, with its continuous Davidic dynasty and central shrine in Jerusalem, was much more politically stable, although its ruler was often forced into vassalage to Israel's king (see 1 Kgs 22). Israel seldom had a ruling family for more than three generations, and there were numerous coup d'etats led by military commanders (see 1 Kgs 16). In addition, the highways that assisted Israel's merchants also allowed foreign armies to march through their territory. Israel will therefore quickly succumb to the growing advance of the Assyrian empire in the eighth century BCE and will be utterly destroyed in 721 BCE by these Mesopotamian rulers. Judah will also be forced to pay tribute and accept Assyrian hegemony, but this smaller, more out-of-the-way country will survive until 587 BCE, when the Babylonian king Nebuchadnezzar destroyed Jerusalem as part of his efforts to crush resistance throughout Syria-Palestine.

51. Why are the actions taken by Jeroboam called "Jeroboam's sin"? (1 Kgs 12:25–33)

Of course, Jeroboam would not have termed as *sin* the policies he crafted in his effort to create a separate identity for the Northern Kingdom of Israel. This label appealed to the editor(s) of the biblical account sometimes referred to as the Deuteronomistic Historian (see questions 5 and 6). These editors from Judah list a series of points that they not only considered to be Jeroboam's sin but also the basis for incorrect, unfaithful behavior by later kings (see 1 Kgs 15:33–34).

First among Jeroboam's sins is his establishment of two shrines that were to rival Jerusalem as religious centers of worship and sacrifice for the Israelites (12:29). They were located advantageously at Bethel (on the southern border with Judah) and at Dan (on the northern border of the kingdom). Both sites already had a history of cultic activity (Bethel is tied to altars built by Abraham and Jacob, and Dan is associated with the idol taken from Micah by the migrating Danites; Judg 18:27–31). Golden calves were shaped and placed in each of these shrines to function as substitutes for the Ark of the Covenant and to symbolize God's presence with the people (1 Kgs 12:28). These images, of course, violate the prohibition of idols in the

Ten Commandments (Exod 20:4–6), but at this stage in Israelite history sacred images are still in fairly common use.

Knowing that he needed to cultivate the support of the local leaders and the people in the villages of Israel, Jeroboam also constructed or sanctioned the use of altars on high places throughout his kingdom. In this way local worship practices could be maintained while the people were required to journey to his conveniently located royal shrines only for major festivals (1 Kgs 12:31a). Of course, there could have been some dissension by the Levitical priests who lived in Israel and whose loyalties might have been attuned to the Jerusalem Temple, but Jeroboam also bypassed them by appointing non-Levitical priests to serve at his royal shrines (1 Kgs 12:31b). Finally, again catering to the local situation and in this case taking into account the differences in climate and harvest calendars in the two kingdoms, Jeroboam shifts the dates of the major religious festivals to entice his citizens to take their offerings to Dan and Bethel instead of Jerusalem (1 Kgs 12:32–33). These strategies all prevented or decreased the flow of Israelite pilgrims to Jerusalem, built loyalty to the centers at Dan and Bethel, and promoted a greater sense of national identity for the newly formed kingdom. However, they did not correspond to the theological beliefs or political loyalties of the southern editors and therefore were judged to be sinful.

52. What "catch phrases" do the editors use in chronicling the reigns of the kings?

The biblical narrative does not contain a complete listing of every accomplishment, good or bad, by the kings of Israel and Judah. The editors of these materials may have worked from regnal archives, but they chose to provide abridged accounts, perhaps due to space restrictions or because their purpose was to make theological judgments about the kings and to point out those monarchs who were either particularly evil (Ahab; 1 Kgs 16:30) or those who were faithful to God's covenant and ruled with justice (Josiah; 2 Kgs 22—23). In order to standardize their work, the scribes and editors injected stock phrases and formulaic statements into the chronicle for each king. For instance, as each king passed from the scene it was common to conclude their account with the statement that he "slept with his ancestors" (1 Kgs 14:20; 16:28), or he was "buried with his ancestors in the city of David" (1 Kgs 14:31; 22:50). For those kings that incurred the ire of God and the editors, their regnal statement included the statement, "he did evil in the sight of the LORD....For he walked in all the way of Jeroboam son of Nebat" (1 Kgs 16:25). Additional formulaic statements that serve as an editor's shorthand are listed below:

Regnal Formulaic Statements

Nadab Nadab son of Jeroboam: "...reigned over Israel two years. He did what was evil in the sight of the LORD, walking in the way of his ancestor and in the sin that he caused Israel to commit." (1 Kgs 15:25–26)

Baasha Baasha son of Ahijah: "...reigned 24 years. He did what was evil in the sight of the LORD, walking in the way of Jeroboam and in the sin that he caused Israel to commit." (1 Kgs 15:33–34)

Elah Elah son of Baasha: "Now the rest of the acts of Elah, and all that he did, are they not written in the Books of the Annals of the Kings of Israel?" (1 Kgs 16:14)

Ahaziah Ahaziah son of Ahab: "...reigned two years over Israel. He did what was evil in the sight of the LORD, and walked in the way of his father and mother, and in the way of Jeroboam son of Nebat, who caused Israel to sin. He served Baal and worshiped him; he provoked the LORD, the God of Israel, to anger, just as his father had done." (1 Kgs 22:51–52)

Jehoram Jehoram son of Ahab: "He did what was evil in the sight of the LORD, though not like his father and mother, for he removed the pillar of Baal that his father had made." (2 Kgs 3:2)

Ahaziah Ahaziah son of Jehoram, king of Judah: "…reigned one year in Jerusalem. His mother's name was Athaliah, a granddaughter of King Omri of Israel. He also walked in the way of the house of Ahab, doing what was evil in the sight of the LORD…for he was son-in-law to the house of Ahab." (2 Kgs 8:25–27)

53. What role does the Elijah and Elisha cycle of stories play in the structure of Kings?

Structurally, the Elijah and Elisha cycle of stories serves as a transition point in the history of Israel. The Northern Kingdom's separation from Judah is now a reality, but the kings of Israel are, according to the Deuteronomistic Historian, doing greater evil than all before them (1 Kgs 16:31–33). Thus, the times need a hero-figure to awaken the people to their obligations to the covenant. To be sure, other prophets appear in the accounts of the kings of Israel prior to the time of Elijah and Elisha (Nathan, Gad, Ahijah), but these two prophetic figures stand out in terms of their ability to confront kings publicly, to perform miracles, and to champion the cause of allegiance to Yahweh and the covenant.

After this time, most of the prophets will be associated with named books and their message is detailed within the context of specific historical events as Israel and Judah are threatened by the encroachment of the Mesopotamian and Egyptian empires. There is also a remarkable connection between their careers and the events during Moses' time as leader of the Israelites. Specifically, both Moses and Elijah/Elisha live during a time of crisis when the people's worship of Yahweh is challenged by foreign gods, and each will have to call upon God's powers over nature to convince the Israelites who the true God is. For example, the devastating effects on the Egyptians by the plagues and the Red Sea crossing in Moses' time can be compared to the confrontation between Elijah and the 450 prophets of Baal on Mt. Carmel that ends with a mighty flash of God's fiery power and the massacre of the Baal prophets (1 Kgs 18).

In a similar way, Moses' repeated intervention in the wilderness that brought healing for afflicted people is comparable to the curing of Na'aman when he follows Elisha's instructions to bathe seven times in the Jordan River (2 Kgs 5:1–19). Both Moses and Elijah have a theophany on Mt. Sinai (meaning Mt. Horeb) that sends them on a mission to serve God (1 Kgs 19:11–18). Plus, they are both able to open up a body of water and cross on dry land (2 Kgs 2:6–8). The tradition of miraculous power and closeness to God make Moses and Elijah/Elisha more than any other prophets truly remarkable figures, and this helps to explain why it is Moses and Elijah that appear to Jesus on the mount of transfiguration (Luke 9:30–33).

54. Why is Jezebel considered the worst woman in Israel's history?

Some would say that evil is in the eye of the beholder. Jezebel's bad press in the biblical account is due primarily to her foreign origins (Phoenician), her use of royal power, and her rather extreme devotion to her god Baal (1 Kgs 16:31–32). A careful examination of the narratives about her also shows that she was a loyal wife and mother and that she was concerned with maintaining the power and authority of the monarchy (see her proud stance in 2 Kgs 9:30–31). However, her methods, which may in part be a reflection of the policies employed in her home country, were by no means diplomatic and could easily be used by the biblical editors against her. For instance, in order to establish Baal worship in Israel, Jezebel convinced King Ahab to build a shrine to Baal in their capital city of Samaria and to erect a sacred pole associated with the goddess Asherah. She also systematically hunted down the prophets of Yahweh in order to eliminate any criticism from that quarter (1 Kgs 18:4, 13).

These actions lead to the confrontation with Elijah at Mt. Carmel in which her 450 Baal prophets were defeated and massacred (1 Kgs 18:20–40). Still, she could command the forces of the army and Elijah fled into the wilderness rather than face her sworn wrath (19:1–4). At another point, when Ahab's neighbor Naboth refuses to sell his land to the king, Jezebel once again displays her foreign attitudes. She sarcastically asks the sulking Ahab, "Do you now govern Israel?" (1 Kgs 21:7) and proceeds to arrange Naboth's judicial murder by bribing two false witnesses (1 Kgs 21:8–14). Once this inconvenience was out of the way (i.e., stoned to death), Jezebel sweetly tells her husband, "Go take possession of the vineyard of Naboth" (1 Kgs 21:15). Such a blatant abuse of power sparks yet another confrontation with Elijah that results in a divine curse of the king and the prediction that Jezebel would ultimately be "consumed by dogs" (1 Kgs 21:21–24). Jezebel was an assertive and strong-willed queen, who was not afraid to use her powers and to manage her husband's affairs. The result is that her name becomes a negative label for a wicked and immoral woman. (See its later symbolic use to condemn a false prophetess in the church of Thyatira; Rev 2:20–23.)

55. Why is Israel in constant conflict with Aram (Syria)?

Conflict between Israel and the various Aramean states begins as early as the reign of Saul in the tenth century BCE (1 Sam 14:47) and continues in the reigns of David (2 Sam 10:6–19) and Solomon (1 Kgs 11:23–25). Since Aram consisted of many minor kingdoms at this early period, it is only later, when Damascus becomes its political center, that Aram becomes a major threat. Thus, throughout the ninth century BCE, as the Northern Kingdom of Israel emerged as an independent state, its chief territorial rival was its contiguous neighbor to the northeast, Aram (Syria). At stake between the two countries were the fertile areas of Gilead and Bashan in Transjordan, as well as control of major trade routes through these areas. Both wanted to maintain a buffer zone and both countries wished to take advantage of the economic opportunities and resources in the region.

The biblical account occasionally makes reference to God's use of Aram to punish Israel for its unfaithfulness and its kings for continuing the policies of Jeroboam (2 Kgs 10:32; 13:3). In the political jockeying that took place, Aram sometimes allied itself with Judah (1 Kgs 15:18–20) and at other times with Israel (2 Kgs 16:5). There are also occasions when a common threat brought all of these smaller states together, as in the case of the Battle of Qarqar (853 BCE), when a coalition led by Hadadezer of Damascus and Ahab of Israel stalled the advances of Shalmaneser III of Assyria. The biblical account, however, focuses its attention on the frequent border skirmishes, as well as on pitched battles between Israel and Aram (1 Kgs 22:29–36). Occasionally the Syrian armies invaded Israel's territory and even besieged the capital city of Samaria (1 Kgs 20:1–6; 2 Kgs 6:24–25). Two Syrian kings are mentioned frequently in the text, Ben-hadad and Hazael. The latter, in particular, was a thorn in Israel's side and he is also prominently mentioned in the Assyrian Annals as a local power. Hazael repeatedly campaigned in Gilead (Amos 1:3–4) and into northern Israel, defeating armies led by Jehu (2 Kgs 10:32–33) and Jehoahaz (813–798 BCE; 2 Kgs 13:1–9). A recently discovered victory stele erected by Hazael at Dan (just north of the Sea of Galilee) claims that he defeated kings of Israel and Judah while gaining control over large areas of northern Israel (compare this to Jehu's claims of victory in 2 Kgs 9:14–26). Competition with Aram was curtailed in the early eighth century after Damascus was captured by the Assyrians. Thereafter, Aram and Israel were allied against the Assyrians, periodically forming alliances with other small states in the region and staging revolts that were bloodily put down by the Assyrian kings (2 Kgs 17:1–6). Both Israel and Aram were finally defeated and their identity as independent nations was ended by the Assyrians after 720 BCE.

56. What extra-biblical sources help with the reconstruction of Israel's history?

Our understanding of the history of the ancient Near East has been enhanced by the discovery of a large number of extra-biblical documents, inscriptions, and royal annals. Some of these texts were produced by officials and scribes in Israel and Judah, but the majority come from the major civilizations in Egypt and Mesopotamia. Each provides an extra piece in the puzzle of recreating the history of ancient Israel and its neighbors. Some provide a measure of corroboration with the biblical account, while others contain material not included by the biblical writers, either because they did not have access to these sources or because these texts contain information that stands in contrast to the viewpoint of the Bible's editors. For example, the rather long account of King Ahab of Israel (1 Kgs 16:29—22:40) makes no mention of the Battle of Qarqar in 853 BCE or the large part Ahab played in the coalition of small kingdoms that fought against Shalmaneser III of Assyria. Such heroics and military skill, however, would be out of place in the biblical account that only features Ahab's foolishness, apostasy, and weakness when it came to his Phoenician wife, Jezebel.

Below is a partial list of major sources used to assist in the study of Israel's history from about 1220 to 535 BCE. The extra-biblical sources are cited in the book *Old Testament Parallels*, abbreviated here as *OTpar*.

Extra-biblical Document	Parallel(s) to Bible	Tie to Israel's History
Merneptah Stele (c. 1208 BCE)— *OTpar*, 97–98	No direct parallel	Egyptian Pharaoh Merneptah lists peoples and cities he conquers in Canaan, including "Israel," providing possible date for Israel's presence in Canaan

Extra-biblical Document	Parallel(s) to Bible	Tie to Israel's History
Mesha Stele (c. 830 BCE)— *OTpar*, 167–689	Josh 6:17–21; 1 Kgs 16:23–24; 2 Kgs 3:4–27	King Mesha details how Moab threw off Israel's oppressive rule; mentions King Omri
Monolith Inscription of Shalmaneser III (853 BCE)— *OTpar*, 178–80	No direct parallel	Assyrian victory stele for Battle of Qarqar; list of Syro-Palestinian kings includes Ahab of Israel
Black Obelisk of Shalmaneser III (841 BCE)—*OTpar*, 180–81	No direct parallel	Assyrian obelisk depicts King Jehu of Israel paying tribute to Assyrian emperor
Tel Dan Inscription (c. 820 BCE)— *OTpar*, 170–71	2 Kgs 10:32–33	Aram's King Hazael describes his defeat of Israel's king Jehoram and the ruler of the "House of David" on stele at Dan
Annals of Sargon II (c. 720 BCE)— *OTpar*, 185–87	2 Kgs 17:5–23	Israel's revolt against Assyria; Samaria captured; Israelites deported
Siloam Inscription (c. 710 BCE)— *OTpar*, 193–94	2 Kgs 20:20	Inscription carved into the water tunnel's wall describing its construction

Extra-biblical Document	Parallel(s) to Bible	Tie to Israel's History
Annals of Sennacherib (701 BCE)— *OTpar*, 190–92	2 Kgs 18:13–16	Record of Assyrian siege of Jerusalem and Hezekiah's ransom to save the city
Arad Letters (early sixth century BCE)—*OTpar*, 198–200	No direct parallel	Short inscriptions on broken pottery record orders to the military garrison in Arad (southern Judah)
Nebuchadnezzar's Annals (598 BCE)— *OTpar*, 195–97	2 Kgs 24:13–17; Jer 29:1–2	Nebuchadnezzar's first capture of Jerusalem
Lachish Letters (587 BCE)— *OTpar*, 201–3	Jer 34:6–7	Judah's garrisons at Lachish report on conditions in the final days before the Babylonians destroyed their post and Jerusalem
Cyrus Cylinder (540 BCE)— *OTpar*, 207–9	Isa 44:24—45:19	Persian royal inscription describes Cyrus's capture of Babylon, release of hostage peoples, the funds to rebuild temples to their gods

57. What is the literary structure and plot of the Second Book of Kings?

The linked episodes that comprise the Second Book of Kings create a narrative covering the period from about 950 to 586 BCE.

Its primary theme is the failure of most of the kings of Israel and Judah to remain faithful to Yahweh and the covenant. This in turn leads to heightened dangers represented by the superpower nations in Egypt and Mesopotamia. The result is a downward spiral that eventually leads to the defeat of both nations (Israel in 721 BCE and Judah in 587 BCE) and to the exile of the people throughout Mesopotamia.

The first nine chapters continue the cycle of stories about the prophet Elisha, his confrontations with the kings of Israel, and the expansion on the "universalism theme" (see 2 Kgs 5) that is intended to make the case that Yahweh is the God of all creation and had also been depicted in Elijah's contest with the Baal prophets on Mt. Carmel (1 Kgs 18). Chapters 10—17 contain short summaries of the reigns of kings in Israel and Judah that include some political details and wars with neighboring states, concluding with the fall of Israel to the Assyrian empire. More attention to the emotional and psychological effect this event has on Judah is found in the prophetic materials, especially Isaiah, Hosea, and Micah. Starting with chapter 18 all attention is focused on the remaining kingdom of Judah (from c. 720 to 586 BCE).

There are two kings (Hezekiah and Josiah) in particular who receive extensive coverage because of their attempts to reform the political and religious character of the nation. They stand in stark contrast to other kings (Manasseh and Jehoiakim), who make no attempt to build upon these reforms and instead allow their Assyrian and Babylonian masters to dictate policy and religious practice in Judah. Judah survives the Assyrian period by paying tribute and not joining the revolts led by alliances of smaller states, although the nation suffers terribly during repeated invasions. The biblical writers use these tragic events to make the point that they are the result of God's anger with an unfaithful people and their leaders (see 2 Kgs 17:7–23; 21:10–15; 24:18–20). In the end, Jerusalem is caught up in the struggle for power between Egypt and Babylonia and is utterly destroyed by Nebuchadnezzar of Babylon in 587 BCE. The account in 2 Kings concludes with the exile of a large portion of Judah's population and much of the nation left in ruins (2 Kgs 24—25).

58. How does the message of Amos and Hosea relate to Israel's history?

Both Amos and Hosea experienced the events in the eighth century BCE that contributed to the demise of the Northern Kingdom of Israel. Amos spoke during the first half of the century when Israel was experiencing a period of peace and prosperity under the rule of Jeroboam II. Assyria had just conquered Damascus and removed Aram as Israel's chief economic and political rival, and the prophet reminded the people and rulers of Israel that their obligation was to thank Yahweh for this turn of fate and to share their prosperity with those less fortunate. When all that the prophet sees is self-serving indulgence (Amos 2:6–8; 4:1–3) and hollow worship-practices (Amos 5:21–24), he warns the Israelites that their "rotten nature" (Amos 8:1–2) will bring a harvest of despair (Amos 8:4–14).

Hosea prophecies during the latter half of the eighth century and may well have been a witness to the capture of Samaria and the exile of Israel's people in 721 BCE. Seeing the impending crisis, the prophet first offers some hope with his marriage metaphor that ends with Yahweh taking back a repentant Israel (Hos 1—3). He warns them like Samuel (1 Sam 15:21) that God demands "steadfast love," not empty sacrifices (Hos 6:4–6), and he points to their sins, for example, the "calf of Samaria" (Hos 8:6; 13:2); multiple altars to other gods (Hos 8:11). Sensing that only harsh words may get through to these rebels against God, Hosea tells them that "they sow the wind and they shall reap the whirlwind" (Hos 8:7). "Bargaining" with Assyria while allying themselves with Egypt and the small states of Syria-Palestine (= their "lovers"; 8:9) can only lead to disaster, and this is precisely what happens when Sargon II of Assyria erases Israel from the table of nations in 721 BCE (*Old Testament Parallels*, 185–87).

59. Who were the Assyrians, and what was their role in Israel's history?

The Assyrians mentioned in the biblical text are in fact the Neo-Assyrian culture that re-emerges in northern Mesopotamia with the reign of Ashur-dan II (934–912 BCE). During most of the tenth century, the neo-Assyrians contested with the Aramean kings for territory in eastern Syria and with the kings of Babylonia to their south along the Euphrates and Tigris Rivers. It is in the ninth century that Assyria and Israel come into contact when Shalmaneser III (858–824 BCE) began to expand his territory to the west and was met at the Battle of Qarqar (853 BCE) by a coalition of kings, including Ahab of Israel, who contributed 2,000 chariots and 10,000 infantry (*Old Testament Parallels*, 179–80). Although temporarily checked by this coalition, Shalmaneser continued to campaign in the region and by 841 BCE he had contained the activities of Hazael of Aram and had received tribute from Jehu of Israel (*OTpar*, 180–81). Political turmoil following Shalmaneser's death provides a period of respite, but then Tiglath-pileser III (745–732 BCE) resumes the Assyrian advance. He becomes the first Assyrian king to be mentioned in the biblical account (Pul in 2 Kgs 15:19) when he exacted a tribute of a thousand talents of silver from Menahem of Israel, and later captured most of the Galilee and northern Transjordan from Pekah of Israel (2 Kgs 15:29).

It will be his successors, Shalmaneser V (726–722 BCE) and Sargon II (721–705 BCE), who will respond to continuing rebellions by Israel's kings by capturing Samaria and deporting its population (722–721 BCE; 2 Kgs 15:30—17:5). With Egypt urging the leaders of the Philistine city-states and the remaining kingdoms in Syria-Palestine to revolt, the Assyrians were required to continually campaign in the region, putting down a revolt led by Ashdod in 711 BCE (Isa 20). King Hezekiah of Judah did not join in this revolt, but his efforts to remove foreign influences over the Temple in Jerusalem and his refusal to pay tribute led to another invasion of Judah and a siege of Jerusalem in 701 BCE by Sennacherib (704–681 BCE; *OTpar*, 191–92). Both 2 Kings 18—19 and Isaiah 36 contain accounts of this siege and the ransom Hezekiah pays to save the city. Throughout Manasseh's reign (696–642 BCE), Judah is a quiet vassal of the Assyrians, but when the last great king of Assyria, Ashurbanipal (668–626 BCE), dies, this opens up general conflict throughout the empire. The Assyrians were defeated in a final battle at Carchemish (605 BCE) by a coalition led by the Babylonians and Medes and they ceased to be a factor in the rest of the history of the ancient Near East.

60. What role did Egypt play in Israel's history between the tenth and sixth centuries BCE?

The tenth to the sixth centuries BCE comprise the Third Intermediate Period of Egyptian history and Dynasties 21 to 26. During this time Egypt is ruled by foreign pharaohs—Libyan (Tanite) and Nubian—and Upper Egypt (southern) and Lower Egypt (northern + delta) were never effectively united under a single ruler. Because of the political divisions that existed, Egypt was not able to exercise the control over Syria-Palestine that had been the case in previous eras. Instead, Egypt plays the role of political provocateur, trying to subvert the loyalties of the petty kingdoms of Syria-Palestine to their Assyrian and later Babylonian masters. In terms of Egypt's interaction with Israel and Judah during these centuries, the biblical account in 1 and 2 Kings and the prophetic materials provide some insight. For example, during Solomon's reign in the mid-tenth century there is a report of a marriage between the king and the daughter of the pharaoh, presumably Siamun (1 Kgs 3:1; 9:16). In addition to the wonderful irony of a leader of a people once enslaved by the Egyptians marrying an Egyptian princess, this report is a clear indication just how fractured Egypt was at the time and how far its fortunes had fallen to make such an alliance.

Perhaps a bit more politically telling are the reports of Solomon's enemies (Hadad the Edomite and Jeroboam ben Nebat) being sheltered by Egyptian pharaohs who saw an advantage to countering Solomon's influence (1 Kgs 11:14–22, 40). When the kingdom of Israel divides in Rehoboam's reign, the pharaoh Shishak (also called Sheshonq) takes advantage by invading the area, setting up a victory stele at Megiddo, and, according to the biblical account, stripping the Temple and palace treasuries in Jerusalem (1 Kgs 14:25–26). This Egyptian incursion is short-lived, and hereafter, most contact with Egypt will be the result of that country's attempt to weaken Assyrian hegemony in Syria-Palestine. Examples include Hoshea of Israel's rebellion against Shalmaneser III (c. 722), refusing to pay tribute and seeking military aid from "King So" of Egypt (possibly Osorkon; 2 Kgs 7:6). The prophet Hosea points to this dangerous political move and warns Israel against such shady diplomatic behavior (Hos 7:11; 12:1).

Similar warnings are given to Hezekiah of Judah by the Assyrian ambassador, the Rabshakeh, who characterizes the Egyptians as a "broken reed…who will pierce the hand of anyone who leans on it" (2 Kgs 18:21; Isa 36:6, 9). The memory of Egypt's duplicity as an ally is recalled in Ezekiel's condemnation of a "staff of reed" that breaks off instead of supports (Ezek 29:6–7). Interestingly, Egypt allies itself with Assyria just prior to the Battle of Carchemish, seeing an opportunity to seize portions of Syria-Palestine; in the process Josiah of Judah is killed when he tries to stop pharaoh Necho II at Megiddo (609 BCE; 2 Kgs 23:29). For a time, Necho controls events in Jerusalem, setting Josiah's son Jehoiakim on the throne (2 Kgs 23:33–34), but he is unable to stop the advance of Nebuchadnezzar of Babylon into the region (2 Kgs 24:7). Some weak efforts are made to support Zedekiah when he revolts against Babylon (Jer 44:30; Ezek 17:15), but when the Babylonians turned from their siege of Jerusalem in 587 to meet the approaching Egyptian army, the Egyptians retreated, leaving Jerusalem to its fate (Jer 37:5, 8). Thereafter, Egypt once again serves as a refuge for exile from Judah (2 Kgs 25:26; Jer 43:1–7), but plays no further part in the politics of Syria-Palestine and is eventually conquered by the Persian army of Cambyses (525 BCE).

61. What are the results of the fall of Samaria in 721 BCE? (2 Kgs 18:9–12)

The immediate result of the fall of Samaria to the Assyrian armies of Sargon II is the extinction of the monarchy in the Northern Kingdom of Israel and the deportation of a large portion of the population to some far region in the Assyrian empire (the unknown area of Halah on the Habor and unspecified cities of the Medes; 2 Kgs 18:11). These deportees will not return to rebuild their nation. Instead, new peoples were brought into Israel from Mesopotamia to repopulate the area and they were eventually schooled in the traditions of that country and its God (2 Kgs 17:24–28; Ezra 4:2). Many refugees must have fled south to Judah after the fall of Samaria, bringing tales of the horrific acts of the Assyrians. It is quite likely that they preserved the prophetic message of Hosea and brought with them the traditions of Elijah and Elisha.

While it is not possible to ascertain the psychological effect of the destruction of the Northern Kingdom on Judah, it is possible to surmise that some saw this as a sign of God's wrath (2 Kgs 17:7–18) and a warning to Judah to keep the covenant. Of course, it also left Judah in a vulnerable position. This small country was invaded and stripped bare of its possessions by a succession of Assyrian campaigns (see prophetic complaints against both Samaria and Jerusalem and their rulers in Mic 1), culminating in Sennacherib's siege of Jerusalem in 701 BCE. Later prophets will continue to point to Samaria's unfaithfulness and demise while pointing out how Judah's failings will lead to similar destruction at God's direction (Jer 23:13–15; Ezek 16:44–58; 23).

62. How does First Isaiah's message relate to historical events in Judah?

An initial time cue is provided in Isaiah's call narrative, "in the year that King Uzziah died" (= 738 BCE). The prophet's confrontation with King Ahaz occurs during the critical moments of the Syro-Ephraimitic War in the 730s when Jerusalem is threatened by a combined army from Israel and Aram. In this instance, Isaiah is instructed by God to meet the king as he and his entourage tour the strategic locations associated with Jerusalem's defenses: "at the end of the conduit of the upper pool on the highway to the Fuller's Field" (Isa 7:3). Thus, when the prophet tells the king that he should leave the city's defenses to the Divine Warrior, it is done in a public place with witnesses, and it forces the king to make a public response. However, Ahaz had already made an appeal to the Assyrians to help him against his neighbors (2 Kgs 16:7).

Because of this, Isaiah then predicts the defeat of Israel and Aram and the impoverishment of Judah as a vassal of the Assyrians, both of which occur when Tiglath-pileser III campaigns in the region (Isa 7:13–25; compare 2 Kgs 16:8–9). During Hezekiah's reign in 711 BCE, Isaiah once again attempts to influence the king by stripping himself naked and proclaiming that the people will become enslaved prisoners of war if they join the revolt against the Assyrians led by the Philistine city of Ashdod (Isa 20). Hezekiah apparently takes this advice, but Judah will be invaded in 701 BCE by the Assyrian emperor Sennacherib after Hezekiah, at the urging of the Egyptians, refuses to pay tribute (2 Kgs 18:13–16). Both 2 Kings 18 and Isaiah 36 record the mocking speech of the Assyrian ambassador, the Rabshakeh, who ridicules Hezekiah's alliance with Egypt (compare Isa 30:1–5). The king is forced to pay a huge ransom to save Jerusalem, but much of the country is devastated by the invading Assyrian army. The report of the death of thousands of the besieging troops and the assassination of Sennacherib by his sons in Isaiah 37:36–38 combines events that did not all occur in the same time frame. Sennacherib's death, recorded in the

Babylonian Chronicle, occurs twenty years after his campaign against Judah.

63. What is the result of Hezekiah's reform movement in Judah?

It is unclear why Hezekiah chose to defy the Assyrians by engaging in a reform movement that cleanses the Jerusalem Temple of foreign influences and strengthens both the monarchy and the priesthood of Yahweh (2 Kgs 18:4). It is possible that he felt his small country was not significant enough to come to Emperor Sargon II's attention during the period between 720 to 705 BCE. To be sure the Assyrians had to deal with repeated revolts in Babylon and the incursions by Urartu on their northern border. Then, when Sargon was killed in battle, it took his successor Sennacherib some time to establish his rule.

All of these factors provided a window of opportunity for vassals on the periphery of the empire, like Judah, to assert their autonomy. What results is an attempt by Hezekiah to remove the local hilltop shrines ("high places") so that greater focus can be placed on the Jerusalem Temple. The elimination of "sacred poles" associated with the goddess Asherah and even the destruction of the bronze serpent—a relic of Moses' intervention for the people in the wilderness (Num 21:8–9)—shows his zeal to adhere to the law against idols (Exod 20:4–6). These acts, coupled with his refusal to "serve" (that is, pay tribute to) the Assyrians and his expansion of his territory at the expense of the Philistine city-states (2 Kgs 18:8), demonstrate his belief that the Assyrians were too weak to respond. However, in his fourteenth year as king (701 BCE), Sennacherib invades Judah. Archaeological excavations have confirmed massive destruction layers at Lachish and other cities as a result of this campaign. Both the biblical account (2 Kgs 18:13–37) and the Assyrian annals (*Old Testament Parallels*, 191–92) indicate that Hezekiah was forced to submit to the emperor and pay a huge ransom to save Jerusalem from destruction.

64. What do the Siloam Inscription, Sennacherib's Assyrian Annals, and the Rabshakeh's speech tell us about the siege of Jerusalem? (2 Kgs 18:13–37; 20:20)

The process of reconstructing events in the history of ancient Israel often includes consulting biblical and extra-biblical written records and inscriptions made available by archaeological excavations. In the case of the siege of Jerusalem by Sennacherib in 701 BCE, there is a wealth of sources to draw on that help fill in gaps and provide a clearer picture of this crisis event. As noted in question 63, King Hezekiah had initiated a number of reforms between 720 and 705 BCE that were aimed at asserting political and cultural independence from the Assyrians. Realizing the possible effect this would have and having firsthand experience of the destructive power of the Assyrians (the fall of Samaria in 721 and the suppression of the Ashdod Revolt in 711 BCE), Hezekiah made preparations for a long siege of Jerusalem. Among these preparations was construction of a water tunnel from the Spring of Gihon outside the city walls to the Pool of Siloam within the city (2 Kgs 20:20).

When this tunnel was discovered by archaeologists in 1880 and cleared of rubble, a Hebrew inscription was found carved into the wall that provides details of its construction (*OTpar*, 194). With his water supply secured, Hezekiah then made an alliance with the Egyptians and assumed that they would support him if the Assyrians invaded Judah. The fact that this assumption was overly optimistic is pounded home to Hezekiah and his political advisers when Sennacherib began to systematically destroy Judah's towns and villages (see Mic 1:8–16). Having cut off supplies to Jerusalem and any foreign support from Egypt (2 Kgs 19:8–13), Sennacherib then sent his ambassador, the Rabshakeh, to dictate terms to Hezekiah. The ambassador's taunting speech is contained in 2 Kings 18:17–35 and Isaiah 36. While the extended biblical account (2 Kgs 19:14–37) contains a divine rescue of Jerusalem, it primarily serves a theological purpose rather than contributing to the historical chronicle. It is more likely that Hezekiah saved his capital by paying a huge ransom (see 2 Kgs 18:13–16). This is corroborated by the account in Sennacherib's royal annals that describe Hezekiah's capitulation and payment of a massive tribute (*OTpar*, 191–92). Although Jerusalem did not fall, Judah was impoverished and during the reign of Manasseh, Hezekiah's son, there is no hint of further rebellion.

65. Why is Manasseh considered the worst king in Judah's history? (2 Kgs 21:1–18)

Manasseh reigned as king of Judah from 696 to 642 BCE. His lengthy rule is due to the fact that he came to the throne at age twelve; this also meant that during his early years policy decisions were made by a group of advisers. Given the fact that the Assyrian emperors during this period are Esarhaddon (680–669 BCE) and Ashurbanipal (668–626 BCE), it was in the best interests of Judah and of Manasseh to quietly accept the terms of their vassalage and give no evidence of rebellion. The royal annals of both of these emperors are filled with their savage suppression of rebellious nations, and the walls of their palace in Nineveh contain lurid portrayals of tortured captives and executed prisoners.

Despite these political realities, the Deuteronomistic Historian classifies Manasseh as the worst king in Judah's history (see 2 Kgs 24:3–4). Every possible charge made against other kings is contained in a scathing indictment of him, including the reversal of Hezekiah's reforms and the construction of altars "for all the host of heaven" in the courts of Yahweh's Temple in Jerusalem, and the erection of a carved image of Asherah (2 Kgs 21:3–8). Like Jeroboam of Israel and the Amorite peoples of Canaan, Manasseh is said to have "misled" the people, taking them away from their loyalty to Yahweh and the covenant (21:9–11). Of course, the editors are writing at least a century after Manasseh's time and their perspective is focused on theological errors, rather than the decisions politicians sometimes must make to preserve the nation from further physical destruction. Still, a bad example can also be used to demonstrate how God is willing to take back even the worst into the fold (compare Hosea's marriage metaphor in Hos 1—3). Thus, in the version of the story in 2 Chronicles 33:10–16, Manasseh prays to God for help and when he receives divine assistance, all vestiges of foreign gods are removed. This account accords with the redemptive hopes of the exilic community and should be seen in that light rather than as a real contribution to the history of Manasseh's reign.

66. What steps does Josiah take to centralize power and authority in Jerusalem? (2 Kgs 23:1–27)

Like his great-grandfather Hezekiah (2 Kgs 18:3–8), Josiah will take steps to remove all vestiges of foreign worship in the Jerusalem Temple, eliminate the "high place" shrines in the local villages, and attempt to expand his territory north into what had been the kingdom of Israel. While couched in terms of religious reform as atonement for the peoples' lack of adherence to the covenant (22:8–13), these were very political initiatives that were intended to centralize power and authority in the monarchy based in Jerusalem. His program of reform began in 622 BCE with the staging of a covenant renewal ceremony before the Temple of Yahweh (2 Kgs 23:2–3). In this way he tied his administration and his reform movement to similar staged events by Moses at Mt. Sinai (Exod 24:3–8) and by Joshua at Shechem (Josh 24:1–28).

Next Josiah made a public show of having the priests strip the Temple of "all the vessels made for Baal, for Asherah, and for the host of heaven" and had these objects destroyed and their ashes cast out with the trash that was strewn in the Valley of Kidron. In this way he reverses Manasseh's policy of religious apostasy (compare 2 Kgs 21:3–7 with 2 Kgs 23:4, 6–7, 10). Such a public demonstration of Judah's independence was made possible by the disintegration of the Assyrian empire after the death of Ashurbanipal in 626 BCE. Then, to insure orthodoxy and centralized control of the entire priesthood in Judah, Josiah deposes local priests who served in the village high places and altars dedicated to other gods (2 Kgs 23:5). Those priests loyal to Yahweh were required to come to Jerusalem where they are given subsidiary tasks and prevented from conducting sacrificial service at local altars (most of which are destroyed on the king's orders; 2 Kgs 23:8).

Basically, Josiah made a clean sweep of every altar, image, and high place that had been dedicated by previous kings of Judah, either removing them or defiling their sacred precinct (2 Kgs 23:11–14). With this done, Josiah turns his attention north, taking his army to Bethel where Jeroboam's royal shrine was destroyed. The tombs of the priests that had served there were defiled (2 Kgs 23:15–16; compare the prophecy in 1 Kgs 13:1–3). Although the text also notes that Josiah removed the high places throughout Samaria, it is uncertain whether he had either the time or the military force to do this before his death in 609 BCE at the Battle of Megiddo.

67. How is Babylon able to come to power amid the ashes of the Assyrian empire?

Reading the royal annals of the Assyrian emperors Esarhaddon and Ashurbanipal raises a question about their success in conquering most of the ancient Near East. These rulers were forced to continually campaign in order to maintain their control or to put down revolts. In particular, they had to pacify Egypt several times between 671 and 650 BCE. Furthermore, the political ambitions of Ashurbanipal's brother Shamash-shum-ukin destabilized Babylonia and eventually contributed to the emergence of Nabopolassar as the ruler of the Chaldean tribes of south central Babylonia.

When Ashurbanipal died in 626 BCE, Nabopolassar took advantage of the opportunity and of the political instability caused by a fight over the succession to have himself declared king of Babylon. With the aid of Media (a growing power northeast of the

Tigris River), he began to systematically drive the Assyrians out of Mesopotamia and dismantle their major strongholds. By 612 BCE, the Babylonian and Median forces had captured and destroyed the Assyrian capital at Nineveh (see Nahum's celebration of this event; Nah 3). Despite Egyptian aid, the Assyrians were driven from Harran in northern Mesopotamia in 610 BCE and crushed at the Battle of Carchemish in 605 BCE by a Babylonian army led by the crown prince Nebuchadnezzar, effectively ending their history as a power in the Near East (see Jer 46:2–12). Nebuchadnezzar succeeds his father in 604 BCE and then resumes his campaigning, driving Egypt out of Syria-Palestine (2 Kgs 24:7), sacking the Philistine city of Ashkelon, and accepting Jehoiakim as his reluctant vassal in Judah (2 Kgs 24:1–2).

68. How is Judah's growing instability depicted in the Second Book of Kings and in the Book of Jeremiah?

The death of Josiah in 609 BCE is the turning point for Judah. His three sons were immediately forced into vassalage or were taken as hostages (2 Kgs 23:31–33). Jehoiakim serves Neco II of Egypt until 604 BCE and then is forced to submit to Nebuchadnezzar of Babylon. Hoping to receive Egyptian support, Jehoiakim revolts in 600 BCE, but he dies during the siege. His son Jehoiachin rules for three months until the city is taken (2 Kgs 24:6–12). Nebuchadnezzar then places Zedekiah on the throne. One sign of how far the kings of Jerusalem had fallen is that as petty kings of Judah, Jehoiakim and Zedekiah are unable to maintain even their given names (2 Kgs 23:31–34; 24:17). Their foreign masters demonstrate their power by renaming them when they are placed on the throne in Jerusalem. The editors of 2 Kings 23—25 choose only to provide an abbreviated account of these final years of Judah's existence. Each king is condemned for his evil ways and his willingness to revolt against Babylonian rule. Thus, two sieges of Jerusalem (600–598 and 588–587) simply result in massive destruction of property and the exile of a large portion of the population.

Nebuchadnezzar utterly destroys Jerusalem in 587 BCE, and when he takes Zedekiah captive, the king's sons are executed and the monarchy is replaced with an appointed governor, Gedaliah (2 Kgs 24:6–22). Jeremiah, an eyewitness to Judah's decline, adds to the history of this period with his warnings of impending invasion (Jer 4:5–8; 6:1–9) and his predictions of doom for each of Judah's kings (Jehoiakim: Jer 36:29–31; Jehoiachin: Jer 22:24–30; Zedekiah: Jer 21:3–7). A clear sense of the desperation of a city besieged by a massive army made up of Babylon and its allies (Jer 25:8–9) is found in Jeremiah's description of the siege ramps and of the danger of pestilence and famine inside Jerusalem's walls (see Jer 32:24). Rather than see them die, he urges them to accept the "yoke of Babylon" (Jer 27:8–11), while maintaining some sense of hope that God would eventually return the exiles to Judah (29:10–14) and that once again they would work the land (32:15, 25). There is no compromise in Jeremiah's message. The people and their leaders must accept the fact that they do not control their own fate. He displays this in graphic enacted prophecies that show that God will not relent in their punishment this time (see Jer 16:1–13).

69. Why does Jeremiah counsel the people of Jerusalem to accept the "yoke of Babylon"?

The political situation between 600 and 587 BCE becomes increasingly more desperate for Judah. When Jerusalem is captured by the Babylonians in 598 BCE and a large group of Judah's citizens are exiled, including King Jehoiachin, it becomes necessary to reconcile these disasters with continued obedience to Yahweh. For some it becomes a test of faith, and false hopes are raised by the prophet Hananiah and others who assure the people that the exile will soon be over, the sacred vessels returned to Jerusalem, and Babylon humbled (Jer 28:1–4; 29:8–9).

Jeremiah, however, repeatedly attempts to make it clear that God's anger will not be quenched so soon. Therefore, Jerusalem and Judah will not escape intact if they continue to rebel against the Babylonians and against God's covenant. In fact, Jeremiah makes it his mission to convince them that Babylon is the instrument of God's punishment (compare Isa 10:5) and that to rebel against Babylon is to rebel against Yahweh (Jer 27:16–22). The yoke or burden placed on them by Babylonian hegemony cannot be broken off the people's neck as easily as Hananiah breaks the wooden yoke off Jeremiah's shoulders (Jer 28:10–11). If they wish to live, then they must surrender to Babylon (Jer 21:8–10), taking on even an iron yoke if God chooses to impose one (Jer 28:14). They are courting disaster if they continue to listen to those who say "peace, peace, when there is not peace" (Jer 6:14; 8:11–12).

70. What are the direct results of Nebuchadnezzar's capture of Jerusalem in 598? (2 Kgs 24)

To begin with, it is important to understand why Jehoiakim revolted against Nebuchadnezzar in 600 BCE. The king of Judah became entangled in the superpower politics of his day, caught between Babylonian and Egyptian interests in Syria-Palestine. When he chose to ally himself once again with Egypt, this created the potential for a general weakening of Babylon's control over that buffer region. A strict lesson was necessary to prevent others from revolting. The result is a siege by an allied army of Chaldeans, Aramaeans, Moabites, and Ammonites that lasts for over a year and ends with Jerusalem falling to an enemy for the first time since David made it his capital (2 Kgs 24:1–2; Jer 25:8–9; 35:11). Without assistance from the Egyptian army (2 Kgs 24:7), Jehoiakim dies during the siege, leaving the throne to his son Jehoiachin, who surrenders the city three months later (24:8–12).

To complete his victory and to prevent another revolt, Nebuchadnezzar takes the sacred vessels from the Temple,

Jehoiachin, members of the royal family, nobles, and high-ranking priests, as well as many of those who could serve in the army as hostages (24:13–16; Ezek 17:12–14). Then he places twenty-one-year-old Mattaniah (renamed Zedekiah) on the throne. Beyond these military and political developments, additional results of Jerusalem's fall are the recognition that the city is in fact vulnerable to attack and that God will not spare the people from this shameful fate (24:24; see this hope expressed in Jer 26:17–19). With so many of the leaders of Judah in exile, those who were left behind cherished hopes of a swift return of these people and the sacred vessels. Some may have chosen to turn to the Babylonian gods when Yahweh seemed to have failed them. Others, like Jeremiah, made the case for acceptance of their punishment as atonement for their refusal to remain loyal to the covenant (see question 69). In any case, Judah's leaders did not learn a lesson and a decade later Zedekiah engages in an ill-considered revolt that leads to the final destruction of the city (2 Kgs 25).

71. How does the message of Ezekiel relate to events in Jerusalem?

Portions of Ezekiel's message make direct reference to the political situation in Jerusalem and the imminent fall of the city. For example, the prophet recounts the fall of Jerusalem in 598, the exile of King Jehoiachin and his court, and the subsequent rebellion of Zedekiah when he chose to rely on Egyptian horses and infantry rather than on Yahweh (Ezek 17:12–21). In Ezekiel 24:1–2, the prophet, who is living among the exiles in Babylonia at this time, notes the date of the siege of Jerusalem in 588 BCE. Then the ultimate fate of King Zedekiah after the walls of Jerusalem are breached by the Babylonians is recounted in Ezekial 12:10–14. Just as 2 Kings 25:4–6 notes, the king attempts to escape the city along with a small armed force. Ezekiel graphically depicts this, portraying Zedekiah carrying his "baggage on his shoulder" and being captured and taken into exile (Ezek 12:12). Several of

Ezekiel's staged prophecies portray the coming siege of Jerusalem (engraved brick; Ezek 4:1–3), the privations suffered by the besieged people (rationed meals; Ezek 4:16–17), and the general destruction of the city's population by sword and fire (shaved head and beard; Ezek 5:1–2).

On a larger scale, Ezekiel's visions provide an explanation for Yahweh's anger with Jerusalem. Most graphic of these is his "out-of-body tour" of the Temple in which he finds the seventy elders burning incense to other gods, women crying tears for the Babylonian god Tammuz, and other abominations defiling the sacred character of the Temple (Ezek 8:7–18). Filled with righteous indignation, Yahweh chooses to abandon Jerusalem to its fate (compare Jeremiah's Temple sermon that warns that God cannot and will not dwell among a people who violate the covenant and in a "house" that is no longer dedicated to Yahweh; Jer 7:3–15). Despite the heat of God's anger, Ezekiel is allowed to say that a righteous remnant would survive the coming storm of destruction by demonstrating their remorse (Ezek 9:3–10; see also 14:21–22). Most devastating of all is Ezekiel's description of the physical departure of the "glory of the LORD" from the threshold of the Temple. A fiery chariot drawn by cherubim transports the deity, leaving behind a hollow shell that will be destroyed by the Babylonians (10:6–22). This destruction is completed at the direction of Yahweh, who declares, "I have set my face against" the city and its people (15:6–8).

72. Why do the people of Judah believe that God will never allow Jerusalem to be destroyed?

To begin with, Jerusalem had not fallen to an enemy attack since David captured the city at the beginning of the monarchy period (2 Sam 5:6–10). Then, when the Assyrian emperor Sennacherib does not capture Jerusalem during the siege of 701 BCE (2 Kgs 18—19), another chapter is added to the myth of inviolability for the city in which God has chosen for his name to dwell (Deut 12:11; 14:23). A Zion theology is developed based on the idea that the Temple Mount (= Zion) was God's "holy habitation" and that the deity would help the city against its foes (Pss 46:4–5; 48:1–8). Of course, this is a revisionist understanding of a crisis situation that impoverished and shamed King Hezekiah. The Assyrians chose to accept a huge ransom rather than extend the siege of a relatively insignificant city.

However, it is clear that Jerusalem's survival is interpreted by later generations in Judah as a sign of divine favor. The tradition of God's concern for Jerusalem is repeated during Jeremiah's trial when village elders cite the case of the prophet Micah's condemnation of Jerusalem (Mic 3:12). They assure the court that, rather than execute the prophet, King Hezekiah took his words to heart and entreated the Lord for help and favor. This in turn caused "the LORD to change his mind about the disaster" and to spare the city. Therefore, the key to survival is to call on God for help in time of trouble (Jer 26:17–19). What the elders did not hear, however, is Jeremiah's call for the people to go to Shiloh, where God's name had originally dwelt and "see what I [God] did to it for its wickedness" (Jer 7:12). Because the city had previously avoided destruction, the assumption was that God would always answer their call even if they were not truly faithful to the covenant. Jeremiah attempted to bust this myth (Jer 21; 25:1–14; 29:17–23; 34:1–7), but until Jerusalem fell and was utterly destroyed in 587, there were some who continued to believe it could never happen (see Zedekiah's plea in Jer 37:1–10).

73. Why does Zedekiah revolt in 588, and what is the fate of Jerusalem in the following year?

From the moment when he was placed on the throne in Jerusalem by the Babylonian king Nebuchadnezzar in 597/96 BCE, Zedekiah was faced with a difficult situation. He had been forced to swear an oath of allegiance promising never to rebel against the Babylonian king (2 Chr 36:13). Yet if he ever hoped to inspire any confidence in his rule and show that he was not just a puppet of a foreign ruler, Zedekiah knew he would have to demonstrate at least some independence of action. This may explain why, shortly after becoming Judah's king, he was willing to host a conference of other subject nations to discuss possible plans for rebellion (Jer 27:3). Although no action was taken for several more years, Zedekiah was apparently bolstered by the hope expressed in the Zion theology (Ps 76:1–3) and convinced that, although Jerusalem had fallen to the Babylonians, God had not abandoned the city and Yahweh's anger would cool (Ps 77:1–9).

This may also explain why he maintains diplomatic relations with the Egyptians and its newly emergent pharaoh, Psammetichus II (595–589 BCE). The pharaoh had recently recaptured control over Nubia and southern Egypt and shown his interest in Palestine by touring the region in 591 BCE. Zedekiah broadened his relations at that point by negotiating for horses and troops from Egypt (Ezek 17:15) and, according to one of the Lachish Letters, sent one of his generals, Coniah ben Elnathan, to visit Egypt on a diplomatic mission (*Old Testament Parallels*, 202–3). Add to this the fact that the Babylonian Chronicle does not mention Nebuchadnezzar visiting Syria-Palestine between 594 and 590 BCE. Zedekiah may have decided the time was right for rebellion while his Babylonian master was occupied with events in the eastern part of the empire. Zedekiah's failure to accurately estimate the political situation is made clear by the fact that only Tyre in Phoenicia and Ammon in Transjordan joined his rebellion (Ezek 21:18–23). Although the new pharaoh Apries (Apries Hophra, 589–570) does send troops into Palestine and this temporarily diverts the Babylonian army away from Jerusalem (Jer 37:1–10), this is not a real attempt by the Egyptians to come to Judah's aid. Zedekiah's and Jerusalem's fates are sealed and there will be no further revolts because the city is destroyed and Zedekiah led away, blinded into exile (2 Kgs 25:1–7).

74. Is Judah an empty land after the fall of Jerusalem?

Because a sizable segment of the population, including the royal court and most of its leaders, was taken into exile between 597 and 586 BCE, Judah is sometimes thought to be an emptied land. The account of Jerusalem's fall in 2 Chronicles 36:15–21, with its blanket statement that the Babylonian king "took into exile in Babylon those who had escaped from the sword," contributes to the myth of an emptied Judah. However, it was the aim of the Babylonians to break the back of rebellion in Judah, not to destroy its economic value as a vassal state on the border with Egypt. An empty land cannot produce taxes and is a political vacuum that is sure to be filled by forces that wish to exploit the region and are antagonistic to the Babylonians. Archaeological evidence actually indicates that the region north and west of Jerusalem did not sustain massive damage and continued to function under the Babylonian appointed administrators.

It is quite likely, in fact, that many of the people who had lived in Lachish, Jerusalem, and sites in south central Judah fled to Gibeon, Mizpah, and other towns to the north, hoping perhaps at some point to return during better times and restore the capital (see 2 Kgs 25:22–25 and Jer 40:7—41:18). Furthermore, when the opportunity arose for the exiles to return to Judah (the Persian province of Yehud) in 538 BCE (Ezra 1), they found it occupied by "the people of the land," descendants of those who had not been exiled as well as others who had settled there (Ezra 4:4; 9:1). The antagonism between the returnees and those they found on their return suggests that the "people of the land" as well as the leaders based in Samaria did not find these "intruders" a welcome sight. This is especially the case given the way that the returned exiles dismiss them from participation in the reconstruction of the Temple (Ezra 4:1–4) and the likelihood that their political and property rights would be brought into question (Neh 1:9–10, 17–20).

PART SIX

Exilic and Postexilic Israel

75. What would life have been like for the exiles in Mesopotamia under Babylonian rule?

The exilic community was created by an unknown number of deportations from Israel and Judah to areas in Mesopotamia. Archaeological evidence does indicate an increase in the number of inhabited or restored sites in Mesopotamia. After the Assyrians destroyed the Northern Kingdom of Israel in 721 BCE, much of its surviving population was deported and apparently succumbed to cultural assimilation. There are references to "Samarians" in the Annals of Sargon II, as well as in economic and legal documents throughout the seventh century BCE, but the exact size of this exilic community and how it was organized is unknown (only the fictionalized Book of Tobit provides a glimpse). Quite likely the majority of these people merged with the surrounding communities and lost their cultural identity. It is possible that the remainder joined the new exilic groups as they were brought to Mesopotamia during the late seventh and throughout the sixth century BCE by the Babylonians.

Ezekiel 8:1 and 33:30–33 suggest that life in exile may have been relatively free of religious persecution and repressive policies. However, the traumatic effects of the deportation (see the anger expressed in Ps 137) and the fact that the Babylonians would expect these new arrivals to mix with the population and become productive members of the empire suggest that it was not a carefree existence. There is evidence from Nebuchadnezzar's annals that he made use of a portion of this labor pool for major building projects. Apparently there were opportunities for members of the *Gôlâh* or exilic community to become farmers, herders, and fishermen, and to use their skills as artisans (something suggested by Jer 29:1–9). The Murashu documents from Nippur in southern Mesopotamia also indicate that some Judean families engaged in economic activities and served as government officials. Of course, to engage in business or to serve in the government would have drawn some to abandon their cultural heritage in favor of blending into their new society (giving their children Babylonian names) and perhaps shifting their attention to new gods.

76. How did the exiles maintain their cultural identity while in Mesopotamia?

For those among the Judean exiles (the *Gôlâh* community) who chose not to assimilate, it became necessary to develop a stronger sense of cultural identity and to define their basic religious and social values. It was also necessary to accept that their violation of the covenant agreement had forced Yahweh to abandon them to their enemies. This understanding—expressed by the prophets Jeremiah (Jer 29:1–23) and Ezekiel (Ezek 33:10–20) as a theodicy or religious rationalization for why God allows events to take a particular course—is a fundamental step in the exiles' theological description of the exile. Coupled with this was the reassurance that the exilic experience could transform them in much the same way that the wilderness experience had transformed the Israelites in Moses' day (see God's promise of a "new heart and a new spirit" in Ezek 18:30–32 and 36:16–36).

Given the strong forces of assimilation that were drawing some of their community away from Yahweh and their Israelite culture, strong measures were necessary to insure their cultural survival, including a complete reformulation of their basic religious and social ideals. They had to rearticulate their identity while taking into account the reality of their current living situation in the exile. A major part of this process was the formulation of the "Jewish Identity Movement," whose elements are listed below. In sum, they pulled together social facets of Israelite belief and tradition while formalizing a set of scriptures, religious practices, and social customs that could combat assimilation and allow both those exiles who chose to remain in Mesopotamia as well as those who eventually return to Yehud a common understanding of what it means to be a member of their community.

Jewish Identity Movement
1. Development of a canon of scriptures to serve the community wherever they reside
2. Use of Hebrew as a liturgical language for religious observances and sacred texts
3. Emphasis on Sabbath worship as a cornerstone of household devotion
4. Circumcision as a means of distinguishing themselves from other communities
5. Emphasis on and enforcement of the Holiness Code to maintain ritual purity through personal hygiene and diet
6. Emphasis on endogamy (marrying only within their own group) to protect cultural integrity

77. What led to Persia's rise and the expansion of its empire in the sixth century BCE?

After the death of Nebuchadnezzar in 562 BCE, no strong successor emerged, and after a palace coup, an unrelated court official and military leader, Nabonidus (556–539 BCE), is placed on the throne in Babylon. Much of what we know of Nabonidus has been written by his political enemies, but it is clear that he made some significant changes in the religious establishment in Babylon, removing Marduk as the city's patron deity in favor of the moon god Sin and diminishing the power of the Marduk priesthood. In addition, Nabonidus's concern with maintaining the Arabian trade routes resulted in his spending ten years (553–543) at Tema in northern Arabia, while delegating his duties in Babylon to his son Belshazzar (Dan 5). As a result of Nabonidus's policies and poor administrative decisions, a political opening was created for Cyrus, the newly emergent ruler of Persia.

Cyrus had begun his career by consolidating his control of the tribal groups in Persia and neighboring Media. In 450 BCE, he began a series of military campaigns in Anatolia that added wealth,

access to the Mediterranean trade routes, and large sections of territory to his growing empire. To complete his conquest of Mesopotamia, he marched on Babylon in 439 BCE. The principal record of
this event is recorded in the Cyrus Cylinder (*Old Testament Parallels*,
208–9). This proclamation is filled with self-aggrandizing propaganda that asserts that Marduk had chosen him to restore his worship in Babylon and to remove Nabonidus from the throne
(compare similar language in Isa 44:24—45:13). It is possible that
Cyrus was assisted in taking the city by the Marduk priesthood and
other disaffected elements within Babylon. Once the Persian king
was safely installed as ruler, he issued a royal decree releasing the
images of the gods that had been collected and held hostage in
Babylon and provided funds to restore their temples. He also gave
the exiles the opportunity to return to their own lands should they
wish to do so. Such a magnanimous gesture helped to quiet the
empire and increase the likelihood that subject peoples would more
readily swear allegiance to the Persians. Subsequently, the reorganization of the empire into administrative units (satraps), the creation
of a messenger system that allowed swift communication, a series of
strong rulers, and the formation of an army that conquered and paci-
fied all of the Near East, including Egypt in 525 BCE, led to the Pax
Persica and a period of stability over the next two centuries.

78. How does Second Isaiah's message parallel the fall of Babylon to the Persians?

The similarity between the language found in Cyrus's victory
proclamation and in Second Isaiah's description of these events is
quite startling. It is likely that the author of this late exilic prophecy,
dating to approximately 538 BCE, had seen or heard Cyrus's document read and then chose to substitute Yahweh's action for the
Babylonian god Marduk in order to demonstrate his belief in the
true God's power. In doing so he effectively provided a theodicy of
these events for the exilic community that was intended to reassure

them that the same God who allowed the exile to occur was now fulfilling his promise to release them (see Jer 29:10–14).

A generation earlier, Ezekiel had used similar language, asserting that God would act to redeem them "for the sake of my holy name" so that the "nations shall know that I am the LORD" (36:22–23). Second Isaiah's version is sufficiently similar to the official Persian account that it adheres to the basic outline of events and provides the same clear sense that the Persian king is acting solely on the command of a god, not for personal ambitions. A final similarity is found at the end of the Cyrus Cylinder that contains the king's efforts to restore ruined temples, return the images of the gods to their shrines, and allow captive peoples to return to their homelands. Where the two documents differ primarily is in Second Isaiah's reiteration that Cyrus does not know it is Yahweh who commands him, while Cyrus is careful to point out to the people of Babylon that it is their patron god Marduk who has sent him (compare the Rabshakeh's speech in Isa 36:10).

Isaiah 44:24—45:1–13	Cyrus Cylinder Account
Yahweh proclaimed Cyrus to be "my shepherd" (44:28) and "his anointed," and an instrument "to subdue nations" (45:1).	Marduk chose ("pronounced his name") Cyrus "and made him ruler of all the earth."
Yahweh promises "to open doors before him" and "break...the doors of bronze" (45:1–2).	Marduk orders a march on Babylon and allows Cyrus to enter the city without a battle.
Yahweh gives Cyrus the victory to demonstrate divine power to him and to all the world: "from the rising of the sun" (45:5).	Marduk induced the people of Babylon to love Cyrus and kings of all the world to bring him their tribute and submit to his rule.
Yahweh proclaims that Cyrus's task includes rebuilding Jerusalem and the Temple (44:28) and setting the exiles free (45:13).	Cyrus orders the rebuilding of ruined sanctuaries and allows captive peoples to return to their former habitations.

79. Did all of the exiles return to Palestine?

In a burst of prophetic enthusiasm, Second Isaiah calls for the exiles to return to Zion (Isa 40:1–11). He assures the people that Jerusalem "has served her term" and that "her penalty is paid" (Isa 40:1). They should not fear, as God brings them from all points of the compass, "everyone who is called by my name" (Isa 43:5–6). Their safety on the homeward trek is assured as God will help them "pass through the waters…and through the rivers," and no flame will touch them when they must "walk through the fire" (Isa 43:2). All this will happen to demonstrate God's glory and power so "kings shall see and stand up, princes…shall prostrate themselves" because God has redeemed the people (Isa 49:7). Such exuberance is to be expected at a time of high hopes for the future and an end of a forced exile (see Ezra 1:5).

However, the spirit expressed here did not move the vast majority of the Jewish *Gôlâh* community to choose to return to Palestine and to resume their life there. Most chose instead to remain in the Diasporic (exilic) communities in Mesopotamia, Persia, and Egypt. During the sixty years of the exile, they had taken Jeremiah's advice seriously and started businesses, purchased land, and established their families (Jer 29:5–9). If they chose to return to their homeland now they could expect to have to start over in a land where they would have to dispute with its current inhabitants for land title. They would be forced to rebuild terraces, plant vineyards, repair ruined homes, and plow fields that had been neglected for generations. For those who did not have a vested interest in returning (priests and political appointees), it would have taken persons of real conviction or adventure to make the decision to go back. As it was, the majority chose not to leave and they eventually formed several vibrant and quite large communities in Egypt and southern Mesopotamia. All told approximately 15 percent of the exiled community did return to Yehud in a series of waves over a period of nearly a hundred years. This movement began in 535 BCE, with a group led by Sheshbazzar (Ezra 1:5–11) and continued periodically at least through about 400 BCE, when Ezra arrived with a newly recruited group of Levites (Ezra 8:1–20).

80. How did life in Palestine/Yehud change under Persian rule?

The return from exile created a divided Jewish community. Those that chose to remain within the Persian domain in Mesopotamia and Egypt continued their struggle to maintain their social and cultural identity while in close proximity to the dominant cultural voice. For those who did return to Palestine, their administration continued to come from Persia, but their identity as a people was reenforced with:

(1) The establishment of a new political entity, the Persian province of Yehud
(2) The restored priestly community and sacrificial cult once the Temple was rebuilt in 515 BCE (Ezra 6:13–15)
(3) Their negative response to overtures by the Samaritans and other neighboring peoples who wished to cooperate on economic and religious matters

These separate forces pulled emergent early Judaism in two directions: In the Diaspora, the Jewish Identity Movement became even more rigid in its adherence to endogamy, dietary laws, and the sanctity of the Torah. In Palestine, where a priestly community had reemerged, cultic legislation (Holiness Code) was formulated and interpreted. In addition, social restraints on some types of cultural interaction (mixed marriages) were relaxed and commercial activity sometimes took precedence over Sabbath restrictions.

What occasionally derailed local custom during those periods was the appearance of Persian-appointed administrators whose intervention took the form of social and legal reform (see Neh 8, 11—13 and Ezra 9—10). Their reform efforts, however, must be understood within the context of Persian imperial policy, which had as its primary goal the maintenance of peace and commercial prosperity within the empire. Local administrators, while given fairly free rein, as compared to Babylonian and Assyrian policy, would still be subject to periodic review as well as charges made by other administrators (see Neh 6:6–7). The peculiar social conditions in which the returned exiles found themselves (long-fallow fields, destroyed towns and villages, and a demographic imbalance that did not consistently provide "suitable" marriage partners) led them to accept greater legal and cultural flexibility.

What solidified the gradually evolving social situation in Yehud was the imposition of Persian imperial policies, which were designed to better define subject peoples and territorial holdings, and the opportunistic efforts of Persian appointees (Diasporic Jews: see Ezra and Nehemiah) to use these policies to aid their attempt to "purify" the nation. To enforce such an ideological change on the community in Yehud, it was necessary to draw upon previously held traditions or to create authentic-sounding precedents for social custom. Thus Ezra and Nehemiah's insistence on endogamy is reenforced by the mandate given to the covenantal community to keep itself separate from the "peoples of the land" (Exod 34:12–16; Deut 7:1–11), and by the custom in the ancestral narratives to marry only within their own social group for the first two generations (Gen 24:3–4; 28:1–5).

81. How does the message of Haggai and Zechariah relate to events in Yehud?

According to the account in Ezra 1:5—4:5 (written over a century after the fact), the early years of the restoration period in Yehud (535–520 BCE) were marked by the return of several groups to the area lead by Sheshbazzar (Ezra 1:8–11) and Zerubbabel (Ezra 2:2), the resumption of worship practices (Ezra 3:1–7), and the laying of the foundation of the Temple in Jerusalem (Ezra 3:8–13). At that point a number of factors contributed to a delay in completing the construction of the Temple. Ezra describes a dispute between Zerubbabel and the "people of the land" over participation in the construction project, which leads to obstruction and the bribing of officials (Ezra 4:1–5).

Haggai, prophesying in 520 BCE, takes this a bit further by condemning the returned exiles for spending time on building "paneled houses" for themselves while letting the Temple of the Lord remain unfinished (Hag 1:4). He points to signs of God's displeasure (failed harvests and a poor economy; Hag 1:5–6) and concludes that their fortunes will not be restored until the Temple is completed. Both Haggai (2:1–9) and Zechariah (4:9–10) call on Zerubbabel and the high priest Joshua to take charge of the construction and complete it so that God will once again bring prosperity to the land. As a Persian appointee, however, Zerubbabel will not take immediate action that will give his political enemies in Samaria and the "province beyond the River" (Tattenai; Ezra 5:3) an opportunity to denounce him. The fact that additional funds had to be requested from the Persian emperor Darius (Ezra 6:1–12) suggests that Cyrus's original bequest had been exhausted and that administrative opposition had been growing to the construction of the Jerusalem Temple since Cyrus's death (Ezra 5:3–17). In addition, the necessity of building houses, cultivating fields, and restoring the economy had obviously taken precedence over the Temple. Ultimately, it will take Darius providing an injection of new funds for the construction to begin again in earnest, and the Temple is completed in 515 BCE (Ezra 6:13–15).

82. Why is there an eighty-year break in the chronicle of Israel's history after the Temple is restored?

From the beginning of Israel's history the biblical text has chronicled the nation's interaction with its neighbors and with the empires that encroached upon their territory from Mesopotamia and Egypt. During the Persian period, Yehud was one of twenty satrapies (provinces) established by Darius. Standard administrative practices in these provinces were intended to maintain stability and order, while insuring that the many different peoples throughout the empire were identified and classified so that the vast Persian bureaucracy could keep track of their affairs and keep the taxes flowing that paid for the imperial ambitions of the emperors. After Darius used his bureaucratic system to check the files and then provide additional funds for the construction of the Temple in Jerusalem (a small expense to pacify the area), there are no official records in the Bible of imperial contact with Yehud until the mid-fifth century when Ezra and Nehemiah are dispatched to the province. The break in the account between 515–440 BCE is based on the relative stability of Yehud during this period and that the Persians had their attention and resources directed toward Greece and other parts of an empire that stretched thousands of miles from India to Egypt and into the Ionian provinces of Anatolia. Quite frankly, Yehud, with a population estimated at only between 13,350 and 20,650 was one of the least significant and most rural units within the larger Persian "province beyond the river" (Ezra 7:21).

Darius and then his son Xerxes tried for the first half of the fifth century to conquer Greece and expand into Europe. However, Darius was defeated by the Athenians at the Battle of Marathon in 490 BCE. His failure and the transition of power after his death sparked an Egyptian revolt in 486 BCE that Xerxes had to suppress. Xerxes then invaded Greece with a huge army comprised of conscripted warriors from throughout his empire, but his initial success, including burning Athens, was offset by his defeat in the naval battle of Salamis in 480 BCE. A costly and basically unsuccessful conflict continued until Xerxes was murdered in 465 BCE, and his successor, Artaxerxes I (465–424 BCE), was forced to deal with yet another Egyptian revolt in 460 BCE. When Greece became embroiled in the Peloponnesian War between Athens and Sparta in 458 BCE, the Persians were able to restore Egypt to the empire and to construct fortresses along all major trade routes. It may be that the difficulties with Egypt restored Persian interest in Syria-Palestine and it is therefore at this point that the biblical narrative resumes when Artaxerxes I appoints Nehemiah as governor of Yehud about 445 BCE (Neh 2).

83. What role did Nehemiah play in the history of Yehud?

Nehemiah plays a dual role in the biblical account of his activities. First, he is the "cup-bearer" of the Persian emperor Artaxerxes I (Neh 1:11), a position that would have brought him into daily contact with the ruler. He is also a member of the Diasporic Jewish community living in the Persian capital of Susa. This helps to explain why a delegation from Judah brought its petition to him asking that the ruined walls of Jerusalem be restored. Nehemiah demonstrates his bureaucratic acumen, his concern for maintaining stability in Yehud, and his willingness to work to benefit his own people by obtaining the appointment of governor, along with letters that grant him passage through the intervening administrative areas (Neh 2:1–8). What becomes clear in the account is that Nehemiah intends to remove the influence in Jerusalem of foreign leaders like Sanballat the Horonite and Tobiah the Ammonite (Neh 2:19). He sees them as political opportunists; this is further demonstrated in his concern over the mixed marriages that threatened, in his mind, the perpetuation of Jewish identity in Yehud (Neh 13:23–28).

After making arrangements to rebuild the citadel (probably to house the Persian garrison) and at least a portion of the wall (Neh 3—4), Nehemiah's efforts are directed at transforming Jerusalem into the political capital of the province, replacing Mizpah, which had served in that capacity since the time of Nebuchadnezzar. To do this, he builds popular support for his regime at the expense of the nobles and the wealthy minority. He ends the practice of making loans at exorbitant interest rates, which had resulted in foreclosures and the sale of Jewish citizens into slavery (Neh 5:1–13). Yet another economy reform closed the gates of Jerusalem on the Sabbath, enforcing its sanctity and demonstrating its importance to Jewish identity (Neh 13:15–22). He took some of the sting out of this order by ending a tax that had been imposed to support the governor's court (Neh 5:14–15). Knowing that he also needed support from the priestly community, Nehemiah made arrangements to restore the Levites to working in the Temple complex and receiving a portion of the tithe. In so doing he diminished the monopoly held by the high priests over this service and these benefits (Neh 13:10–14, 30). While he is not directly mentioned in the effort to increase the population of Jerusalem (Neh 11:1–2), it is logical that by magnifying the city's importance he contributed to its desirability as an urban center. Nehemiah served two terms as governor and set a tone of vigorously upholding Jewish identity and rejecting cultural or political compromise.

84. Who are the Samaritans?

The answer to this question is complicated by a lack of reliable archaeological and textual information. When the Northern Kingdom of Israel was conquered by the Assyrian king Sargon II in 721 BCE, a large portion of the population was deported and new peoples from Babylon, Cuthah, Avva, Hamath, and Sepharvaim were brought in to populate the cities of Samaria (2 Kgs 17:24). Although not all of the Israelites were removed, their descendants continued to call themselves Samaritans and to worship Yahweh. When Jerusalem was destroyed by Nebuchadnezzar and many of the Judeans were taken into exile in 586 BCE, another group of the people left behind lived primarily in the northern area of Judah and Benjamin with their administrative center at Mizpah (2 Kgs 25:22–23). These people in both Samaria and Judah, who did not experience the exile, are referred to as "the people of the land" in Ezra 4:4 and are characterized as opponents and adversaries of the returned exilic community in Yehud.

For instance, Sanballat the Horonite (Neh 2:10, 19) is referred to in the Elephantine Papyri as governor of Samaria (see *Old Testament Parallels*, 214). His rhetorical sparring with Nehemiah over the reconstruction of Jerusalem's walls and his alliance with

Tobiah the Ammonite indicate both political jealousy and a concern that Jerusalem will eclipse Samaria as the principal center in that region. There is evidence later in the late fifth and early fourth centuries BCE of the construction of a rival shrine by the Samaritans at Mt. Gerizim near Shechem, and this is coupled with a clear theological division between the two groups, with rival priesthoods in place (see Sir 50:26). Their rivalry continues into the Hellenistic period and eventually results in the destruction of the Gerizim shrine in 128 BCE by the Hasmonean king Hyrcanus. The polarized attitudes that divided Jews and Samaritans continue into the Roman period and are apparent in the story of the "Good Samaritan" (Luke 10:29–37).

85. What role did Ezra play in the history of Yehud?

Ezra functions as a scribal expert on Jewish law sent by the Persian emperor Artaxerxes II in 398 BCE to Jerusalem to teach and enforce that law and to insure social and political stability in the province of Yehud (see the embedded decree of the king in Ezra 7:11–28). Unlike Nehemiah, who arrived with an entourage of Persian cavalry (Neh 1:9), Ezra leads a group of Levites and other members of the Diasporic community in an apparent recreation of the Exodus from Egypt (Ezra 8). On arrival he immediately takes up his task as adjudicator of compliance with the laws by denouncing mixed marriages, proclaiming that the "holy seed has mixed itself with the peoples of the lands" (Ezra 9:1–3). His shame, fasting, and weeping over this practice demonstrate the conservative, orthodox attitude of the Diasporic Jewish community and their prejudice against any person who had not experienced the exile (Ezra 9:5—10:1; compare the portrayal of Moses' grief in Deut 9:18). Eventually, he commands the leaders of "the returned exiles" (Ezra 10:16) to swear an oath to annul these mixed marriages and thus purify the community of foreign influences (Ezra 10:4–43).

More important than this forced social cleansing, however, was Ezra's staging of a covenant renewal ceremony (Neh 8:1–12), the fourth in the history of ancient Israel (see Exod 24:3–8; Josh 24:1–28; 2 Kgs 23:1–3). His solemn reading of "the book of the law of Moses" before the Water Gate in Jerusalem (Neh 8:1) closes a chapter in the history of the nation and reiterates their obligation to the covenant now provided for them in written form. Since it was written in Hebrew, the Aramaic-speaking populace was assisted by Levites "to understand the law" thereby setting a precedent for its interpretation by those trained in the Law (8:7–8). The incorporation of a general confession expressed by those present, the signing of the sealed document, and the affirmation thereafter that they "will not neglect the house of our God" serve in an idealized way as Ezra's crowning achievement in the shaping of the religious character of Yehud and by implication future generations (Neh 9—10).

86. What is the literary structure and plot of the Books of Chronicles?

The Books of Chronicles are divided into three sections. First Chronicles 1—9 provides an introduction to the origins of the Israelites in the form of extensive genealogies, ranging from Adam through the household of Saul. The longest section of the Chronicler's work recounts the united monarchy under David and Solomon (1 Chr 10; 2 Chr 9). The depth of detail in this section indicates the belief that this period comprised a sort of golden age in the nation's history. Finally, 2 Chronicles 10—36 consists of an abbreviated history of the three centuries of the Judahite monarchy, including contacts with the Northern Kingdom founded by Jeroboam and concluding with Cyrus's release of the exiles (2 Chr 36:22–23).

The basic themes contained in these sections are the constancy and faithfulness of God and God's mercy in the face of the apostasy and disobedience of the Israelites. The inclusion of the genealogies in the initial section of the work provides both a basic family tree and—to the ancient audience—a clear picture of the identity of the Israelite people. In addition to the political details of David's and Solomon's reigns in section two (including an almost idyllic sense of harmony between the tribes and the Davidic monarchy), great attention is given to portraying the construction of the Temple and the establishment of the cultic patterns of Temple worship led by the priests and Levites.

Following Solomon's death, the idealized political situation is transformed by the division of the kingdom and instances of both reformers (Hezekiah in 2 Chr 29—32, and Josiah in 2 Chr 34—35) and recidivists like King Ahaz, who violated the covenant with his idolatries and was "given into the hand of the king of Aram" by an angry God (2 Chr 28:1–7). The conclusions drawn from divine requital, however, are instructive and redemptive rather than simple punishment. Thus the destruction of Jerusalem and the exile are seen as an opportunity for transformation and hope, with Cyrus serving as God's tool in engineering the return of the exiles (2 Chr 36).

87. How does the account of Israel's history in the Books of Samuel and the Books of Kings differ from that in Chronicles?

The team of biblical editors collectively known as the Chronicler, writing in the late fourth century, reshapes the History contained in Samuel-Kings to fit their political and theological understanding of the history of Israel. While the Chronicler was familiar with and drew upon the earlier Deuteronomistic history and other sources in the compilation of events, it consciously chose to leave some events out of the narrative and the result is a rather whitewashed version that omits any negative material about David and Solomon. To illustrate this, let us compare the Chronicler's version with the Deuteronomistic Historian's recital of the events that lead up to the secession of the northern tribes.

In Samuel-Kings it is very clear that Solomon's apostasies (building shrines for his foreign wives' gods) are a prime cause of the division of the kingdom. The political crisis is also the result of Rehoboam's diplomatic failures and his unwillingness to negotiate with the tribal elders at Shechem (1 Kgs 11—12:19). Since Ahijah had already designated Jeroboam as the future king of the Northern Kingdom (1 Kgs 11:29–39), it was a simple matter for the elders to turn to Jeroboam as their leader and secede from the united monarchy. In contrast, the Chronicler did not wish to place any blame on Solomon or on any Davidic king. Instead, the explanation for the division of the kingdom is included in a "call to return" speech delivered by Abijah, Rehoboam's son (2 Chron 13:4–12). Abijah points the finger at Jeroboam and the "worthless scoundrels" (= the elders) for taking advantage of Rehoboam, who is characterized as a young, inexperienced ruler, who "could not withstand them" (13:6–7). The argument is made that Jeroboam's traitorous actions and the breaking away of the northern tribes are totally illegal since they ignore the everlasting covenant established by God with the House of David (13:5). The chart below provides additional examples in which the Chronicler's version varies with that in Samuel-Kings:

Events in Samuel-Kings	Events in the Chronicler's Account
Saul's narrative (1 Sam 9—30) contains his entire reign with both positive and negative material included.	The only material on Saul's reign is found in 1 Chronicles 10 and focuses on his final battle, death, and his unfaithfulness.
David dances unclothed before the Ark as it enters Jerusalem and has a confrontation with Michal (2 Sam 6:14–23).	These episodes are omitted in the narrative in 1 Chronicles 16.

Solomon made a house for Pharaoh's daughter, but there is no mention of denying her the right to dwell in "the house of David" (1 Kgs 7:8).	Solomon builds a separate house for his Egyptian wife since she could not dwell in "the house of David" because "the places to which the ark of the LORD has come are holy" (2 Chr 8:11).
Manasseh is portrayed as the worst king in Judah's history and a cause of Judah's fall to Nebuchadnezzar (2 Kgs 21:10–15; 23:26).	Manasseh is portrayed as a repentant sovereign and reformer (2 Chr 33:1–9), who could not be blamed for Jerusalem's fall to the neo-Babylonians.

88. Are First and Second Chronicles, Ezra, and Nehemiah a literary unit?

The argument has been made that the full history developed by the Chronicler begins with 1 Chronicles and ends with Ezra-Nehemiah. Bolstering this position is the fact that 2 Chronicles 36:22–23 concludes with Cyrus of Persia's conquest of Babylon and his decree that the Temple in Jerusalem be rebuilt and that those exiles who wish to return to their land may do so. Ezra 1:1–4 begins with this decree and then proceeds to tell a portion of the story of the returned community in Yehud. Even though there is evidence that they sometimes employ common source material (compare 1 Chronicles 9 and Nehemiah 11), have a similar style of writing, and make extensive use of genealogies, there are sufficient differences between these works to question single authorship.

For example, Chronicles uses genealogies to link Israel to the many descendants of Abraham and in the process takes note of numerous instances of intermarriage (Judah's Canaanite wife in 1 Chr 2:3, as well as other examples in 2:17, 35; 3:2). This contrasts with the strong denunciations of intermarriage in Ezra 9:1—10:44; Nehemiah 10:30; and 13:23–28. Furthermore, the characterization of the Davidic monarchy in Chronicles focuses primarily on the positive political accomplishments of David and Solomon and the faults of their successors, the construction of the Temple, and the structuring of the priestly community. Ezra-Nehemiah, when it dwells on the now-defunct monarchy, points to King David's role in the setting of precedents for worship practice and music (Ezra 3:10 and Neh 12:24). Ultimately, it is probably best to see the inclusion of the Cyrus decree in both 2 Chronicles and Ezra as an editorial device intended to provide a link between two different works. By treating each book separately, it is possible to consider these pieces of postexilic literature on their own merits and perhaps learn more about what they can tell us about the social and religious attitudes in this period of Jewish history.

PART SEVEN

Hellenistic and Roman History

89. What do we know about Jewish communities outside of Yehud?

While a relatively small Jewish community was reestablishing itself in Jerusalem and Yehud during the fifth century BCE, much larger Jewish communities existed in Mesopotamia, Persia, and Egypt. During the Babylonian exile, some structure was established for these communities as they engaged in farming and business (see Jer 29:5–7). As time went on, their cultural identity was defended against assimilation by the formulation of the Jewish Identity Movement (see questions 76 and 80) and the continuation of the leadership of the elders (Ezek 8:1; 14:1–5; 20:1). The fact that the majority of these exiles of the Diasporic community chose not to return to Yehud suggests that they had made a good life for themselves; the Murashu documents that mention Jews engaged in a wide range of business practices add to this impression. For those who fled to Egypt (Jer 42—43:7), their descendants migrated throughout the land. The personal and business correspondence from the Jewish garrison on the island of Elephantine in southern Egypt indicates a desire by this fifth century community to maintain contact with Jerusalem and to continue their worship practices even in the face of the destruction of their Temple by their hostile neighbors (*Old Testament Parallels*, 210–15).

The most important Jewish community in Egypt flourished during the Hellenistic period (third to first century BCE) in the important Nile Delta port city of Alexandria. It will be their desire to have a canon of scriptures in their commonly used Greek language that will produce the Septuagint translation, and they remain a large and dynamic ethnic enclave for centuries (see the first-century CE Jewish historian Josephus, *The Jewish War* 2.495). There is also evidence of Jewish presence in cities all around the Levant, from Antioch in Syria throughout Asia Minor and into Greece and in Rome (Acts 2:9–11). Connections and pilgrimages continue between these far-flung communities and Jerusalem until the destruction of the Temple in 70 CE.

90. What role does Alexander the Great play in the history of Israel?

Alexander of Macedon came to power in 334 BCE, after the assassination of his father Philip II. Marshaling support from the Greek states in his capacity as leader of the League of Corinth, he mobilized an army of 40,000 infantry and cavalry to liberate the Ionian cities of Asia Minor. Eventually, Alexander's need to destroy the Persian navy by capturing its ports all along the Mediterranean coast led to victories over Tyre and Gaza, as well as his acceptance in Egypt in 332 BCE of the title of pharaoh, with its implied designation as a god-king, the son of Zeus-Ammon. Fighting continued until 330 BCE when the Persian emperor Darius III is assassinated and Alexander proclaims himself "Lord of Asia" (see 1 Macc 1:2–4). Never satisfied with expanding his territory and always desirous of surpassing the accomplishments of earlier conquerors, Alexander spent the remainder of his life campaigning in India and the eastern provinces of Persia. His increasing tendency to adopt Persian court manners and dress caused a rift with his Macedonian troops and commanders that might have ended in a major breach if Alexander had not died in 323 on the eve of an expedition into Arabia.

On the whole, Alexander the Great's conquests will facilitate a two-way cultural exchange, with Greek culture blending with the ideas and religions of the East. His success in bringing all of the Near East under one rule and his claims to divinity set the stage for the Roman conquests four centuries later. In terms of the history of Israel, Alexander's armies ended Persian rule but he chose to retain much of the administrative structure they had put in place. After his death, Alexander's generals divided up the newly formed empire, with Ptolemy claiming Egypt and Palestine. Later conflicts between the successors of Ptolemy and another general,

Seleucus, will result in the transference of Syria-Palestine to the Seleucids in 200 BCE. Even more important than these political changes, however, is the initiation of a new cultural era in which Judaism struggled to accommodate with Hellenism. Alexander had brought philosophers, architects, and other representatives of Greek culture with him on his campaigns. As a result, in the newly established cities like Alexandria in Egypt and in major urban centers throughout the empire, it became a general practice to put in place the basic elements of Greek city planning, intellectual activities, and social attitudes that form the basis of the Hellenistic culture (see questions 91 and 92).

91. What is Hellenism?

Hellenism is the blending and sharing of cultures between the Greek world and various peoples in the ancient Near East, beginning with the increased trading links during the Persian period and accelerating after the conquests of Alexander of Macedon. The settlement of Macedonian soldiers in colonies throughout the Near East and the establishment of a Greek-dominated political structure in the successor states (some like the Ptolemies in Egypt, taking on the Near Eastern model of divine kingship) established by Alexander's generals also contributed to this process, but it will be almost a century later that the non-Greek population will be allowed entrance into many Greek associations like the gymnasium or into government posts.

As a hybrid culture Hellenism is characterized by:

(1) the use of Greek as a lingua franca for business and eventually everyday speech by both Greek and non-Greek peoples (a by-product being the translation of the Hebrew Bible into the Greek Septuagint in Alexandria, Egypt)

(2) the adoption of the Greek city-state model (the *polis*) as the standard for urban administrative units

(3) the incorporation of Greek education and architectural forms for public buildings, gymnasia, and city planning

The Hellenistic age is also noted for the large increase in immigration from Greece to take advantage of the burgeoning economy and government jobs available in the successor states founded in Egypt and Mesopotamia. These individuals brought with them a desire to maintain a Greek-like lifestyle through education, literature, and recreational opportunities, but they were also just as willing to borrow or adopt Middle Eastern religions and dress when it suited their purposes. With the magnification of foreign trade that resulted from the managed economies and standardized coinage of the Ptolemaic government in Alexandria, the degree of cultural diffusion increased and introduced new ideas and products as well as new inventions that increased productivity (Sir 38:29).

One particularly good example of the growing synthesis in the Hellenistic world was the combination of Greek and Babylonian astronomical mathematics that eventually allowed them to calculate the relative positions of the planets, an essential tool for those concerned not only with science but with the zodiac. The shared cultural heritage created by Hellenism can also be found in the growing number of references to Greek philosophy found in the writings of Jewish historians such as Josephus, Philo, and Aristobulus, whose aim was to broaden an appreciation for Jewish traditions and moral thought within the wider Mediterranean cultural area.

92. What influence did Hellenism have on Palestine?

The degree to which individuals were influenced by the Hellenization of Palestine and the rest of the ancient Near East and Mediterranean world depended in large part on their individual social situation. For peasants working the land, it is unlikely that they were Hellenized to any great extent. They would continue to speak Aramaic, to associate with their limited social group, and to operate within time-honored institutions. Their primary contact with the larger culture would come when they paid their taxes in Greek coinage or produce to whichever political regime was in charge, depending on whether the Ptolemies, the Seleucids, or the Hasmoneans controlled their area, or when they visited Jerusalem for the major religious festivals. If a person wished to take advantage of the increase in commerce ushered in during the Hellenistic period or to rise in importance in the major urban centers, it became necessary to adopt Greek manners, acquire a fluency in the Greek language, have his children schooled in Greek education, and perhaps give them Greek names.

It should also be noted that the competition between the Ptolemies and the Seleucids for control of Palestine (reviving the age-old struggle between the superpowers of Egypt and Mesopotamia) does complicate the lives of many of the Jews. When the Seleucids win the Battle of Panion in 200 BCE (Josephus, *Jewish Antiquities* 12.132), their greater insistence on the introduction of Greek culture will lead to some social upheavals. For some, like the high priests Menelaus and Jason, advocating the transformation of Jerusalem into a Greek *polis* and the construction of gymnasia will serve as an opportunity for the advancement of their own careers (1 Macc 1:11–15; 2 Macc 4:7–34). Others whose ideas and anger are expressed in the deuterocanonical books of 1 and 2 Maccabees find the growing shift toward Hellenistic practices a reason to revolt against their Greek masters in the name of Jewish orthodoxy (1 Macc 1:20–2). Still, it would be a mistake to think that a Jew could not be a Hellenizer. Judaism is a religion and it can be practiced in the midst of any other culture; for example, the pious Jewish writer Philo of Alexandria who wrote in Greek while maintaining a strict adherence to Jewish practice and belief. What can be said is that the diffusion of Hellenistic culture did influence the politics of Palestine and transform the economy. While this did lead to some polarization between those Jewish groups who adhered to strict orthodoxy, others were not so quick to condemn Hellenism. The second-century Jewish scribe Ben Sira is clearly familiar with Hellenistic culture, providing advice on proper etiquette at banquets (Sir 31:12—32:13) and warning against the avarice that comes from seeking gold (Sir 26:29—27:3). As a person who aspired to serve the powerful of his day, he advocates caution, respect, a clear understanding of honor, and fear of the Lord (Sir 7:6; 10:19–25; 20:28; 39:4). None of these ideas rejects Hellenistic culture, but they do indicate a concern for the retention of religious and social values.

93. What is the literary structure and plot of the Books of Maccabees?

The deuterocanonical First and Second Books of Maccabees provide a continuation of the history of Yehud and Jerusalem during the Hellenistic period and in particular the period from 200–63 BCE. They chronicle the Maccabean Revolt beginning in 168 BCE and the subsequent establishment of the Hasmonean Jewish kingdom. First Maccabees, with its pro-Hasmonean agenda and liberation theme, can be divided into four sections:

(1) An introduction that details the rise of Antiochus IV and his repressive measures against the Jews and the Temple (1:1—2:70)

(2) The campaign led by Judas Maccabeus to drive out the Seleucids and restore Jewish religious practices (3:1—9:22)

(3) The rise of Judas's brother Jonathan as the struggle continues (9:23—12:53)

(4) The liberation of the citadel under a third brother, Simon, who is proclaimed both king and high priest (12:24—14:15)

The Second Book of Maccabees retells the story of Judas's revolt. In this version, more details are provided about the Hellenizing efforts of the high priests Jason and Menelaus (2 Macc 4:7–29), and more attention and emphasis are given to events surrounding the Temple in Jerusalem, including its desecration, eventual rededication, and the inauguration of the festival of Hanukkah (2 Macc 4:1—10:9). Further disturbances are described in 2 Maccabees 10:10—15:37 involving threats to Jerusalem by neighboring kingdoms as well as the infighting over the control of the Temple. Throughout these troubles God repeatedly intervenes to defend the Temple and to provide Judas with a succession of victories (2 Macc 10:29–30; 11:8; 15:20–28).

94. How did the struggles between the Ptolemies and Seleucids affect Israel's history?

Following the death of Alexander of Macedon, several of his generals carved out successor kingdoms for themselves. Two of the most important to Israelite history are Ptolemy, who claimed Egypt, Palestine, and the Syrian coastal plain, and Seleucus, who acquired northern and eastern Syria, Asia Minor, and portions of upper Mesopotamia. Both of these men will proclaim themselves to be divine rulers, in the same manner as Alexander, but Egypt tended to be a much more homogenous area to control than Seleucus's domain. In fact, Ptolemy and his successors created one of the most efficient state economies of all time, increasing international trade and commodity production and then squeezing businessmen, farmers, and temple communities with heavy taxes. This in turn created a strong upper class who formed the basis of Ptolemy's royal bureaucracy in every province of his tightly controlled kingdom and produced such wealth that Ptolemy and his successors could afford to engage in a series of five wars of expansion with the Seleucids between 280–200 BCE.

Interest in Jewish apocalyptic sources in this struggle is evidenced in the references to the kings of the north and south in Daniel 11:5–9. Palestine, like every other administrative unit, benefited from economic growth, but at the expense of high taxes. The Temple in Jerusalem was treated like other temple cities, watched over by state officials, but otherwise given a measure of autonomy to conduct worship in its own manner. There does seem to be a

growth of unrest and resentment between the rural and urban population given the differences in status and wealth.

Our best source for Ptolemaic economic and political policy
is the archive of an Egyptian official named Zenon, who traveled
for a year in Syria-Palestine inspecting facilities and determining
how best to exploit resources for the king. This included making
alliances with some local Jewish nobles like the Tobiah family, who
later led a pro-Seleucid party against the Ptolemies and energized
the level of conflict within Palestine around 220 BCE in the hope
of gaining support from the Seleucid ruler Antiochus III. Still, the
Seleucids were not able to make lasting inroads into the Ptolemaic
forces in Palestine until the accession of a boy-king, Ptolemy V
Epiphanes, who is controlled by his advisers and weakened by the
growth of independent power among the Egyptian priesthood.
Antiochus took advantage of the situation to once again precipi-
tate a war that quickly resulted in a Seleucid victory at Panion in
200 BCE and his claim of all Palestine as his domain. His subsequent decrees issuing tax exemption for several influential groups
in Jerusalem were intended to increase his control and solidified
the authority of the pro-Seleucid high priest Simon (Sir 50:1–21).
Antiochus's victories led him into unwise ventures in Greece that
brought him into too-direct contact with the growing Roman
presence there, and his defeat at the Battle of Magnesia in 190 BCE
resulted in loss of territory and heavy debts.

Following a period of weak Seleucid rulers and sensing an
opportunity to gain greater power in Jerusalem, the Tobiah family
offered to pay increased tribute and a large bribe to the newly
crowned Antiochus IV in 175 BCE in exchange for the appointment of the Hellenizer Jason as high priest (2 Macc 4:7–10). From
this point, Antiochus IV's military failures and his need for funds
contributed to the internal struggles in Jerusalem for control of the
Temple, its wealth and influence. The excesses of Jason and his successor Menelaus (2 Macc 4:11–29) and Antiochus's decree ending
circumcision and desecrating the Temple (2 Macc 6:1–11) con-

tribute to an uprising led by Judas Maccabeus and the eventual expulsion of the Seleucids from Judea.

95. What were the causes and results of the Maccabean Revolt?

To begin with, it must be noted that the Maccabean Revolt was not simply a conflict between Hellenism and Jewish culture. While the Hasmonean family that led the revolt were traditionalists and upholders of the basic tenets of Jewish law and exclusivist worship of Yahweh, they would not condemn Hellenism, and in fact make use of the Greek rhetorical and diplomatic forms in their dealings with Rome and with the Seleucids (1 Macc 12:1–4). What seems to have contributed the most to the revolt are the reforms of the high priests Jason and Menelaus and the anti-Jewish policies of Antiochus IV. The polemical account of these events in 2 Maccabees 4:7–17 describes Jason's efforts to further Hellenize Jerusalem as a Greek *polis* (2 Macc 4:9) with the construction of gymnasia and the introduction of public games and Greek fashions.

After Menelaus bribed his way into the office of high priest, his greed and outright theft of sacred objects from the Temple (2 Macc 4:39–50; 5:15–16) contributed to social unrest and may have contributed to Antiochus's later punitive policies against the Jews. In any case, it sparked further disputes between the influential families in Judea, who were already divided by pro-Seleucid versus pro-Ptolemaic political alliances. Once Antiochus staged armed attacks on Jewish citizens (2 Macc 5:24–26) and introduced his anti-Jewish policies that defamed Temple worship and proscribed Jewish practices like circumcision (1 Macc 1:41–50; 2 Macc 6:1–6), one of these major Jewish families, the Hasmoneans of Modein, would call for open resistance and revolt (2 Macc 8:1–4). The revolt has some initial success under the leadership of Judas Maccabeus, but it stalls in 161 BCE when he is killed; it will not be until 152 that Judas's brother Jonathan emerges as a new leader of the rebel forces.

What ultimately turned the tide and gave the Hasmoneans a final victory that removed Seleucid control over Jerusalem and Judea is their ability to patch together a coalition of disparate interest groups (see 1 Macc 2:42) to keep the fighting going and thus cost the Seleucids more than they cared to spend on this province. In addition, the internal struggles for power among the Seleucid nobility weakened their resolve and ability to organize an effective military response. The result is the establishment, under the third Hasmonean brother, Simon, of an independent kingdom (1 Macc 13:31–42) with the Hasmonean monarchs taking on a dual role of king and high priest even though Simon was unrelated to David or to the Zadokite priesthood (1 Macc 10:18–21). While this was a source of tension among the Jews, it seems to have been offset by Hasmonean policies that preserved Jewish monotheism (1 Macc 9:73; 14:25–49; 2 Macc 10:1–8) and autonomy until the Romans replace the Seleucids in 63 BCE as the power in Syria-Palestine.

96. How do the stories and visions in the Book of Daniel relate to events in the Hellenistic period?

Although portions of the Book of Daniel, especially the heroic tales in chapters 1 to 6, predate the Hellenistic period, it seems likely that the apocalyptic dream visions in chapters 7 to 12 and the final editing of the entire book took place in the second century BCE. There are sufficient allusions to historical events involving the struggles between the Ptolemaic and Seleucid kingdoms and to the repression of the Jews in Jerusalem and Judea in December 167 BCE, during the reign of Antiochus IV, to make this probable. Furthermore, references to the "four kingdoms" and especially to the mixture of iron and clay in Daniel 2:36–45 date this vision to the period after the creation of the Ptolemaic and Seleucid kingdoms.

While it is possible to point to the trials faced by Daniel and his three friends at the Babylonian court as models for proper behavior and as an argument against cultural assimilation during the exile as well as in the Hellenistic era, there is no way to make direct connections with Antiochus's decrees. For instance, Nebuchadnezzar's erection of a massive statue and his demand that all of his subjects bow down and worship this golden idol on pain of death (Dan 3:1–7) could be compared to Antiochus's threats to kill anyone who fails to obey his decrees that were intended to transform worship in the Jerusalem Temple (1 Macc 1:41–50). But this is only a literary parallel. In contrast, the recitation of Daniel's visions does have direct connections with Hellenistic political history and with Antiochus's heavy-handed policies. Still, they must have been composed prior to 164 BCE since there is an incorrect prediction of the death of Antiochus IV in Israel (Dan 11:40–45).

Antiochus IV's Decree	References in Daniel to Antiochus's Reign
The result of Antiochus's decree is that "people could neither keep the sabbath, nor observe the festivals of their ancestors" (2 Macc 6:6).	Dan 7:24–25 details the internal conflicts among the Seleucids that led to the reign of Antiochus IV and notes his efforts to "change the sacred seasons and the law."
Antiochus orders his representatives to "defile the sanctuary and the priests," build altars to other gods, sacrifice swine, forbid circumcision, and make the people "abominable by everything unclean and profane" (1 Macc 1:46–48).	Dan 11:20–28 describes the rise of a "contemptible person" obtaining the kingdom by intrigue, and his forces (compare the "little horn" in 7:8 and 8:9–12) "shall occupy and profane the temple" and abolish regular offerings while setting up "the abomination that makes desolate" (Dan 11:31; see Dan 9:27).

97. What do we know about the Hasmonean rulers of Israel?

The formal establishment of the autonomous Jewish state under the rule of the Hasmoneans begins in 142 BCE. Simon, the last of the original Hasmonean brothers, rules until his murder in 135 BCE, and with the accession of his son John Hyrcanus (135–104 BCE), this became a hereditary monarchy until its demise with the coming of the Romans in 63 BCE. What becomes clear from our sources is that the Hasmonean rulers drew on as many sources of power as possible to maintain their control of the state. These included serving as both king and high priest, maintaining a standing army both to defend the crown and to engage in an almost-constant series of wars of expansion, and making diplomatic overtures with Rome and Sparta in order to keep the Seleucid rulers from either invading or destabilizing their regime.

At its height, under Alexander Jannaeus (103–76 BCE), the Hasmonean kingdom had expanded north to the Galilee region, east as far as Nabatea, and to the Mediterranean coastal city of Gaza. Non-Jewish populations were forced to convert, depart, or pay significant tribute. When the Hasmonean rulers became more concerned with increasing their wealth and authority, leaving behind the ideals of the original movement that had sparked the Maccabean Revolt, they turned to the wealthy and influential Sadducean party for support. This also produced new opposition movements, including the Pharisees, an offshoot of the pious *Chasidim*, who vocally opposed the policies of the king and were persecuted for their activities. Toward the end of the Hasmonean period, the monarchy degenerated into fratricidal warfare with multiple claimants to the throne, cries for land reform, and disparate interest groups competing for Rome's favor. The Roman general Pompey exploited these divisions and, using the excuse of treachery by one prince, he captured Jerusalem, transforming the nation into a Roman tributary.

98. How do the Romans become the rulers of Palestine?

The Romans were particularly adept at taking advantage of other nations' weaknesses and playing one group off another. Opportunity knocks when Alexander Jannaeus's widow, Salome Alexandra (76–67 BCE), succeeds her husband as ruler of the Hasmonean kingdom. This requires her to share power with the Pharisees, who are given control of domestic affairs, and to remain dependent upon the Sadducees, who control the army. Her two sons, Hyrcanus and Aristobolus, will soon begin jockeying for the right to become her heir. All of these various factions contribute to internal destabilization while the threat of invasion by the Armenian king Tigranes adds danger to the diplomatic/military picture.

When Tigranes allied himself with Mithridates of Pontus (Asia Minor), this provided Rome with an excuse to invade Armenia in 69 BCE, forcing Tigranes out of Syria and leaving the weak Seleucid ruler unable to avoid Roman vassalage. Salome's death in 67 BCE brought on a succession crisis with the brothers forming competing armies and the Sadducees and Pharisees taking sides. Hyrcanus also received support for his claim from Antipater, the governor of Idumea (father of Herod), and the Nabatean king Aretas III. Sensing a chance to solidify his political strategy of creating a bulwark of vassal states along the rim of the Mediterranean as a protective buffer against the Parthian kingdom in Mesopotamia and Persia, the Roman general Pompey stepped in as a broker in this dispute. After determining that Hyrcanus was the weaker of the two brothers and therefore easier to control, Pompey subjected Aristobolus to a series of negotiations that eventually resulted in the signing over of all fortresses in Judea to the Romans. When Aristobolus and his Sadducean supporters tried to prevent Pompey from entering and taking control of Jerusalem, a siege took place, ending in a massacre of 12,000 Jews (*Psalms of Solomon* 8; pseudepigrapha) and the placement of the former Hasmonean kingdom into the administrative hands of the Roman governor of Syria in 63 BCE.

99. What role is played by the Sadducees, Pharisees, and Essenes?

The majority of what is known about the Sadducees, Pharisees, and Essenes comes from the work of the first century CE Jewish historian Josephus. He is by no means an objective historian and therefore much of what is said must be taken with caution. The Pharisees and Sadducees appear to be competing parties starting in the Hasmonean period, and they both become embroiled in the complex political and religious arguments of that era. What seems to distinguish them is that the Sadducees were most influential among the wealthy classes and had a great deal of power over the Temple priesthood (Josephus, *Jewish Antiquities* 13.298). They rejected any law other than that of Moses (*Antiquities* 13.297) and denied the possibility of life after death (Acts 23:8).

The Pharisees appear to be primarily nonpriests, although some are known to have served on the Sanhedrin council. They advocated theological positions that included expanding the Law to include interpretative traditions of scribes and sages, the resurrection of the dead, and the need to maintain strict purity. They also opposed the combined monarchy and high priesthood of the Hasmonean rulers, and this brought them into conflict with John Hyrcanus and Alexander Jannaeus (see *Antiquities* 13.291–298).

In contrast to these two politicized groups, the Essenes formed separatist communal groups like the one at Qumran designed to avoid all luxury and to exercise self-control with a daily regimen of prayer, work, ritual purity, and strict observance of the Sabbath (Josephus, *The Jewish War* 2.119–161). The Essenes were only a small group, perhaps 4,000 members. Some aspects of their interests in the study of scripture and their speculations on the power of fate and immortality of the soul are contained in the Qumran Rule of the Community and other sectarian texts.

100. What role does Herod play under Roman rule?

Herod's father Antipater is responsible for the family's initial rise as Rome became the master of Syria-Palestine. Antipater's support of Julius Caesar led to an appointment as procurator of Judea (*Jewish War* 1.187–194), and he was able to appoint his sons Phasael and Herod as governors of Jerusalem and Galilee respectively. Herod also made use of the Roman civil war to advance his fortunes and wrest Jerusalem from the Jewish aristocracy. Under the patronage of Mark Antony, he was confirmed as "king" of the Jews in 37 BCE, a title that did not hide his role as a client of the Romans. To insure his control of the throne, Herod engaged in a reign of terror, executing his political opponents, appointing non-Jews and Idumean relatives to high positions, and ending the hereditary high priesthood by appointing his own candidates.

When the conflict between Antony and Octavian broke out, Herod was quick to change sides and offer his services to the future Augustus Caesar in 30 BCE (*Jewish War* 1.386–397). With this new patron, Herod expanded his control over the entire area once ruled by the Hasmoneans. He honored the Romans by dedicating temples to their gods, sponsoring public games, renaming cities, or building new ones like the coastal port of Caesarea Maritima and Sebaste (formerly Samaria). This both flattered his masters and contributed to the growth in economic prosperity in his realm. He created a Hellenistic court so lavish that no other vassal ruler in the Near East rivaled his display or energy. It was during this period of stability that Herod also began the construction of numerous public buildings, a magnificent palace, and the massive new Temple to Yahweh in Jerusalem. Despite these cosmopolitan gestures, Herod never felt entirely safe, spent great amounts on fortresses throughout the country, and dealt savagely with his political rivals, many members of his own family. He served as a valuable ally of Rome for 33 years, but in his later years he became mentally unstable and this contributed to difficulties over the succession and greater control of the area by the Roman governors.

101. Why did the Romans find it so difficult to administer Palestine?

The administrative structure within the Roman Empire consisted of three classes of provincial governors, depending on whether a province was considered "safe" or potentially troublesome because of a strong indigenous culture that had demonstrated a willingness to rebel in the past. Those, like Judea after 6 CE, were under the direct control of the emperor and were assigned a military presence along with a procurator. The official residence of the procurator in Judea was Caesarea. In addition to the collection of taxes (Luke 2:2), this official exercised judicial authority and controlled all military garrisons of auxiliary troops within the province, positioning them around the country to deal with local uprisings or to police major cities like Jerusalem during festival times. A limited autonomy was granted to local authorities, allowing them to deal with ordinary civil and criminal cases, although the procurator retained the right to use capital punishment (Matt 27:15–23; Luke 23:13–25).

In administering Judea, however, the procurators found that it was necessary to respect Jewish religious customs and to exempt the people from the emperor cult. Pontius Pilate, more insensitive to these local customs than his predecessors, sparked conflict when he ordered Roman troops to bring their standards with an engraved image of the emperor into Jerusalem (Josephus, *Jewish Antiquities* 18.3.1). Strained relations between the Jews and the Roman government, resulting from pogroms in Alexandria and threats of erecting a statue of the emperor Caligula in the Jerusalem Temple, were quelled for a time when Claudius appointed Herod's grandson Agrippa with control of Judea and Samaria in 39 CE. Even so, internal dissent over the transformation of Judea into a Roman province continued to break out, led by resistance fighters called the Zealots, who advocated the exclusive sovereignty of Yahweh and freedom for the country (Acts 5:36–37; *Antiquities* 18.1.6). Their refusal to accept the political situation, unlike the Pharisees who tended to collaborate with the Romans, kept the area in turmoil and cost the Romans in unpaid taxes and military expenditures.

After the death of Agrippa, provocations increased during the administration of procurators, who were quick to break up crowds and took bribes allowing the Zealots to proclaim additional charges of tyranny and religious bigotry against the Romans. It is clear that constant turnover of officials, too much latitude for individual action in this fringe province (plundering the Temple treasury), and either ignorance or insensitivity to local custom all contributed to the turmoil. Outright revolt occurs in 66 CE, led by a coalition of resistance groups, including Zealots as well as some of the leaders of the Jewish priesthood. After three years of warfare throughout the country, nearly one-third of the Jewish population was killed or enslaved, Jerusalem was captured and Herod's Temple totally destroyed in 70 CE. The final stage was the siege of the Zealot stronghold of Masada in the Judean desert in 74 CE. The sacred vessels from the Temple were paraded through Rome's streets as part of a triumphal procession for Titus, marking an end to Jerusalem as a Temple city and requiring a reorientation of Judaism away from the priesthood and the sacrificial cult and toward rabbinic leadership in local communities.

Select Bibliography

General Reference

Achtemeier, Paul J., editor. The *HarperCollins Bible Dictionary*, revised edition. San Francisco: Harper & Row, 1996.

Brisco, Thomas C. *Holman Bible Atlas: A Complete Guide to the Expansive Geography of Biblical History*. Nashville, TN: Broadman & Holman, 1999.

Freedman, David N., editor. *The Anchor Bible Dictionary*. New York: Doubleday, 1992.

Meyers, Eric, editor. *The Oxford Encyclopedia of Archaeology in the Near East*. New York: Oxford, 1997.

Rainey, Anson F. and R. Steven Notley. *The Sacred Bridge: Carta's Atlas of the Biblical World*. Jerusalem: Carta, 2006.

Sakenfeld, Katherine D., editor. *The New Interpreter's Dictionary of the Bible*. Nashville, TN: Abingdon, 2006.

Sasson, J. M., editor. *Civilizations of the Ancient Near East*. New York: Scribners, 1995.

Walton, J., V. H. Matthews, and M. Chavalas. *The IVP Bible Background Commentary: Old Testament*. Downers Grove, IL: InterVarsity, 2000.

Histories of Ancient Israel

Ahlstrom, Gösta W. *The History of Ancient Palestine from the Paleolithic Period to Alexander's Conquest*. Sheffield, UK: Sheffield Academic Press, 1993.

Lemche, Niels P. *Ancient Israel: A New History of Israelite Society*. Sheffield, UK: JSOT Press, 1988.

Matthews, Victor H. *A Brief History of Israel*. Louisville, KY: Westminster/John Knox, 2002.

Miller, J. Maxwell and John H. Hayes. *A History of Ancient Israel and Judah*, second edition. Louisville, KY: Westminster/John Knox, 2006.

Provan, Iain W., V. Phillips Long, and Tremper Longman, III. *A Biblical History of Israel*. Louisville, KY: Westminster/John Knox, 2004.

Schäfer, Peter. *The History of the Jews in Antiquity*. Luxembourg City, Luxembourg: Harwood Academic, 1995.

Soggin, J. Alberto. *A History of Ancient Israel*. Philadelphia: Westminster, 1984.

Ancient Near Eastern Texts in Translation

Josephus, Flavius. *The Works of Flavius Josephus*. William Whiston, translator. New York / Edinburgh: T. Nelson and Sons, 1883.

Hallo, William W. and K. Lawson Younger, Jr. *The Context of Scripture* (3 vols). Leiden, Netherlands: Brill, 1997–2003.

Matthews, Victor H. and Don C. Benjamin. *Old Testament Parallels: Laws and Stories from the Ancient Near East*, third edition. Mahwah, NJ: Paulist Press, 2006.

Pritchard, James. *Ancient Near Eastern Texts Relating to the Old Testament*, third edition. Princeton: Princeton University Press, 1969.

Additional Works

Ben-Tor, Ammon, editor. *The Archaeology of Ancient Israel*. New Haven: Yale University Press, 1994.

Borowski, Oded. *Agriculture in Ancient Israel*. Winona Lake, IN: Eisenbrauns, 1987.

Campbell, Anthony F. and Mark A. O'Brien. *Unfolding the Deuteronomistic History*. Minneapolis: Fortress, 2000.

Collins, John J. *Jewish Wisdom in the Hellenistic Age*. Louisville, KY: Westminster/John Knox, 1997.

Dever, William G. *What Did the Biblical Writers Know & When Did They Know It?* Grand Rapids, MI: Eerdmans, 2001.

Dorsey, David A. *Roads and Highways of Ancient Israel.* Baltimore: Johns Hopkins University Press, 1991.

Finkelstein, Israel. *The Archaeology of the Israelite Settlement.* Jerusalem: Israel Exploration Society, 1988.

Grabbe, Lester. *Judaism from Cyrus to Hadrian.* Minneapolis: Fortress, 1992.

Halpern, Baruch. *The First Historians: The Hebrew Bible and History.* San Francisco: Harper & Row, 1988.

King, Philip J. and Lawrence G. Stager. *Life in Biblical Israel.* Louisville, KY: Westminster/John Knox, 2002.

Kuhrt, A. *The Ancient Near East, 3000–330 BC.* London: Routledge, 1997.

Lemche, Niels P. *The Israelites in History and Tradition.* Louisville, KY: Westminster/John Knox, 1998.

Matthews, Victor H. *Studying the Ancient Israelites: A Guide to Sources and Methods.* Grand Rapids: Baker Academic, 2007.

——— and Don C. Benjamin. *The Social World of Ancient Israel.* Peabody, MA: Hendrickson, 1993.

Mazor, Amihai. *Archaeology of the Land of the Bible.* New York: Doubleday, 1992.

McNutt, Paula. *Reconstructing the Society of Ancient Israel.* Louisville, KY: Westminster/John Knox, 1999.

Nakhai, Beth A. *Archaeology and the Religions of Canaan and Israel.* Boston, MA: ASOR, 2001.

Redford, Donald B. *Egypt, Canaan, and Israel in Ancient Times.* Princeton, NJ: Princeton University Press, 1992.

Richard, Suzanne, editor. *Near Eastern Archaeology: A Reader.* Winona Lake, IN: Eisenbrauns, 2003.

Schwartz, Seth. *Imperialism and Jewish Society, 200 B.C.E. to 640 C.E.* Princeton: Princeton University Press, 2001.

Sicker, Martin. *Between Rome and Jerusalem: 300 Years of Roman-Judaean Relations.* Westport, CT: Praeger, 2001.

Snell, Daniel. *Life in the Ancient Near East*. New Haven: Yale University Press, 1997.

Commentaries

JOSHUA

Boling, Robert G. *Joshua*. New York: Doubleday, 1982.

Butler, Trent C. *Joshua*. Waco, TX: Word, 1983.

Creach, Jerome F. D. *Joshua*. Louisville, KY: Westminster/John Knox, 2003.

Hawk, L. Daniel. *Joshua*. Collegeville, MN: Liturgical Press, 2000.

Hess, Richard. *Joshua*. Downers Grove, IL: IVP, 1996.

Nelson, Richard. *Joshua*. Louisville, KY: Westminster/John Knox, 1997.

Woudstra, Marten H. *The Book of Joshua*. Grand Rapids, MI: Eerdmans, 1994.

JUDGES

Boling, Robert G. *Judges*. New York: Doubleday, 1975.

Matthews, Victor H. *Judges/Ruth*. Cambridge: Cambridge University Press, 2004.

McCann, Clint. *Judges*. Louisville, KY: Westminster/John Knox, 2003.

Niditch, Susan. *Judges*. Louisville, KY: Westminster/John Knox, 2008.

Schneider, Tammi. *Judges*. Collegeville, MN: Liturgical Press, 2000.

SAMUEL

Anderson, A. A. *2 Samuel*. Dallas: Word, 1989.

Brueggemann, Walter. *First and Second Samuel*. Louisville, KY: Westminster/John Knox, 1990.

Cartledge, Tony W. *1 & 2 Samuel*. Macon, GA: Smyth & Helwys, 2001.

Klein, Ralph W. *1 Samuel*. Waco: Word, 1983.

McCarter, P. Kyle. *1 Samuel*. New York: Doubleday, 1980.

————. *2 Samuel*. New York: Doubleday, 1984.

KINGS

Cogan, Mordechai. *1 Kings*. New York: Doubleday, 2001.

———— and Hayim Tadmor. *2 Kings*. New York: Doubleday, 1988.

Gray, John. *1 & 2 Kings*. Louisville, KY: Westminster/John Knox, 1970.

Hobbs, T. R. *2 Kings*. Dallas: Word, 1986.

Jones, G. H. *1 & 2 Kings*. Grand Rapids, MI: Eerdmans, 1984.

Nelson, Richard. *First and Second Kings*. Louisville, KY: Westminster/John Knox, 1987.

Sweeney, Marvin A. *I & II Kings*. Louisville, KY: Westminster/John Knox, 2007.

Wiseman, D. J. *1 & 2 Kings*. Downers Grove, IL: IVP, 1993.

CHRONICLES

Braun, R. *1 Chronicles*. Dallas: Word, 1986.

Dillard, R. *2 Chronicles*. Dallas: Word, 1986.

Japhet, Sara. *I & II Chronicles*. Louisville, KY: Westminster/John Knox, 1993.

Klein, Ralph W. and Thomas Kruger. *1 Chronicles*. Minneapolis, MN: Fortress, 2006.

Knoppers, Gary N. *1 Chronicles 1—9*. New York: Doubleday, 2004.

————. *1 Chronicles 10—29*. New York: Doubleday, 2004.

Tuell, Steven S. *First and Second Chronicles*. Louisville, KY: Westminster/John Knox, 2001.

Williamson, H. G. M. *1 and 2 Chronicles*. Grand Rapids, MI: Eerdmans, 1982.

EZRA-NEHEMIAH

Blenkinsopp, Joseph. *Ezra/Nehemiah*. Louisville, KY: Westminster/John Knox, 1988.

Clines, D. J. A. *Ezra, Nehemiah, Esther*. Grand Rapids, MI: Eerdmans, 1984.

Davies, Gordon. *Ezra and Nehemiah*. Collegeville, MN: Liturgical Press, 1999.

Fensham, Charles. *The Books of Ezra and Nehemiah*. Grand Rapids, MI: Eerdmans, 1983.

Thorntveit, Mark. *Ezra and Nehemiah*. Louisville, KY: Westminster, 1992.

Williamson, H. G. M. *Ezra and Nehemiah*. Dallas: Word, 1985.

MACCABEES

Goldstein, Jonathan. *1 Maccabees*. New York: Doubleday, 1976.

——. *2 Maccabees*. New York: Doubleday, 1983.